LETTERS FROM A DEAD MAN
"He sought the secrets of the Pole; he found the secrets of God."

Thus reads the epitaph of ROBERT FALCON SCOTT whose last diaries were the only surviving remnant of a heroic 1910 expedition to the South Pole. CHARLES A. TINDLEY rose from slavery to become a self-taught classical scholar, preacher, and composer of international renown. GEORGE BENNARD was the man behind THE OLD RUGGED CROSS, yet his greatest pride lay in the Gospel, not in the hymns which made him famous. JOHN CALVIN exercised leadership in the growing Reformation movement which was started by the great Reformer MARTIN LUTHER. DAVID LIVINGSTONE chose Africa over the honor and comforts of civilization, and in death closed the slave markets of Zanzibar forever. His own days were numbered, but WILLIAM WILBERFORCE liberated the enslaved populations of the British Empire, helping to end one of the vilest eras in his country's history.

Their greatest weapon was their faith; THEIR FINEST HOUR changed our lives.

THEIR FINEST HOUR

Charles Ludwig

David C. Cook Publishing Co.
850 NORTH GROVE AVENUE • ELGIN, IL 60120
In Canada: David C. Cook Publishing (Canada) Ltd., Weston, Ontario M9L 1T4

THEIR FINEST HOUR

Copyright © 1974, David C. Cook Publishing Co.

All rights reserved. Except for brief excerpts for review purposes, no part of this book may be reproduced or used in any form or by any means—electronic or mechanical, including photocopying, recording, or informational storage and retrieval systems—without written permission from the publisher.

David C. Cook Publishing Co., Elgin, IL 60120

Printed in the United States of America
Library of Congress Catalog Number: 74-82112

ISBN: 0-912692-45-6

*For the memory of
L. Richard Burnap—
great friend, great
editor, great Christian.*

CONTENTS

1	*God's Willing Slave*	13
2	*The Martyr of Prague*	20
3	*Old Rugged Cross*	27
4	*End of a Feud*	32
5	*The Salvation of the Old Blasphemer*	38
6	*The Secrets of the Pole*	45
7	*"Here I Stand"*	51
8	*Robert Moffat and the Outlaw*	57
9	*The "Peculiar" Preacher*	63
10	*The Absent-Minded Poet*	68
11	*The Inflexible Man*	75
12	*The Shrimp Who Grew*	83
13	*The Bedridden Dynamo*	90
14	*"Let Us Go On"*	97

List of Illustrations

Plate

Dr. Charles Tindley I
Stone relief of John Hus II
Monument to John Hus II
George Bennard III
Mr. and Mrs. Frank Virgil III
William Hatfield IV
Robert Falcon Scott V
John Newton VI
John Newton's church VI
Dr. Martin Luther VII
Robert Moffat VIII
Tapestry of Dutch family VIII
Jager Afrikaner IX
John Calvin and William Farel X
Robert Sheffey XI
William Cowper XII
Catherine and William Booth XIII
William Wilberforce XIV
Medal honoring William Wilberforce XV
Model of a slave ship XV
Tree carving where Dr. David Livingstone's heart
    was buried XVI
Dr. David Livingstone XVI

Credits

Appreciation is expressed to the following publishers for permission to reprint articles that first appeared in another form in their magazines.

The General Commission of Chaplains and Armed Forces Personnel, Washington, D.C., for: "George Bennard and His Famous Hymn," Copyright 1967; "John Hus: Martyr," Copyright 1967; "He Had a Cause," Copyright 1972; "He Sought the Secrets of the Pole," Copyright 1968; "He Rode by Faith." Copyright 1970.

World Vision: "Robert Moffat and the Outlaw," Copyright 1968.

Herald Press: "Faraday, the Preacher Scientist"; "He Sang in the Night"; "Amazing Grace"; "The End of a Feud."

Scripture Press: "The Chariot Is Coming." Copyright 1960.

Wesleyan Publishing House: "Charles Tindley—Preacher."

Graded Press: "David Livingstone's Finest Hour." Copyright 1971.

1

God's Willing Slave

At age 17, former slave Charles A. Tindley could read and write only one word—*cat*. Nevertheless, before his death he mastered Greek and Hebrew, preached regularly to four thousand, and was repeatedly asked to become a bishop. His hymns are still known throughout the world.

Tindley's first squint at life was not pleasant. He was born into plantation slavery on Maryland's eastern shore, and lost his mother when he was only five. Then his owner separated him from his father and sold him to a man in a nearby city. Thus, early in life, he learned the meaning of heartbreak.

His new owner, perhaps noticing the spark of genius in his eyes, forbade him to learn to read or to go to church. Literate slaves might consider such revolutionary ideas as the equality of men, so he determined not to have any literate slaves.

But trying to control Tindley's mind was like trying to

bind a lion with a charred rope. Occasionally he found an old newspaper or a torn page from a book. He carefully hid these treasures, for he dared not even glance at them in public. Then, long after the other slaves had gone to sleep, he would take out his papers and try to unscramble the strange markings by candlelight.

Once freedom was attained after the Civil War, Tindley could no longer be barred from church services. But getting to church—any church—was extremely difficult. Generally he would start walking to Chesapeake Bay by early Saturday morning. As he drew near, he would scrub his only shirt, using ashes for soap. The moment it had sufficiently dried on a tree limb, he was ready to step boldly into the little frame meetinghouse.

As he began to understand the mysteries of reading, he became more and more determined to get an education. Working the fields in the scorching sun was back-breaking, yet he was never too tired to walk fourteen miles each evening to learn his three R's. Sometimes he was so tired when he got home he could barely stagger through the door and flop, fully dressed, into bed.

Soon he moved to Philadelphia, where he earned his living as a church janitor and hod-carrier for three years. He began to take correspondence courses, determining to learn at least one valuable bit of knowledge each day. At first he just wanted to accumulate knowledge, but after his conversion he studied with a purpose. He wanted to be a minister.

Studying for the Methodist ministry with little or no background was extremely difficult. "You'll never make it, Charlie," his friends said glumly, shaking their heads.

Tindley, however, wasn't worried. For although his only diploma was a worn-out broom, he spent every spare dollar on books. Moreover, he devoured them, crunched their bones, and made them a part of himself. Eventually the final exams were announced, and to the astonishment of nearly everyone, he was second highest in the class. He then accepted the pastorate of a tiny Negro church at Cape May—an obscure crossroads in southern New Jersey.

Cape May could not hold him long. Soon he was summoned to Philadelphia.

The Bainbridge Methodist Church where he had formerly janitored was nothing to brag about. It was a mere storefront mission that could barely pay its bills. Those in the know predicted soon and sudden failure. Tindley, however, was challenged; and when he was faced with "impossibilities" he just called on the Lord.

Soon the mission was crowded, and a sanctuary seating six hundred was purchased. But even this was not large enough for the eager crowds, so the congregation installed a balcony that would take care of another two hundred. Still, it wasn't big enough.

Tindley now began to have higher hopes. In spite of bitter opposition, he led in the purchase of an old building that had been used by a white congregation. The building seated fifteen hundred.

"His eyes are bigger than his mouth," said some as they withdrew their support. But so many people came that Tindley was forced to post a notice requesting his people to attend only once on Sunday! Tuesday prayer meetings alone averaged one thousand.

But the more he begged people not to come, the more they came. Finally, it was decided to enlarge the old building so that it would seat thirty-two hundred. To do this, they had to purchase and dismantle five neighboring houses. The cost was a whopping $350,000—an incredible amount for a congregation made up of either former slaves or the children of former slaves. But Tindley knew how to invoke enthusiasm.

Dedication was set for Sunday, December 7, 1924. It was a day of anticipation for the entire city. However, it was also the day Mrs. Tindley died. It was a shattering blow, for there were a number of small children. Tindley, however, took it in his stride. He was an old hand at dealing with heartbreak.

His fantastic courage drew the people, and the building was jammed three times every Sunday. Within almost no time there were seven thousand members, and his buildings at South Broadway and Fitzwater became a Philadelphia landmark.

Honors began to move his way. His days were filled with speaking engagements. On one occasion he spoke in a building alive with clergymen, editors, educators, and even a few bishops. As he faced them in the humility that never deserted him, he said, "I am not worthy to speak to such a distinguished congregation as this." Then, while he led in prayer, he prayed, "Father, speak through me as if I were a telephone; and when you are through hang up."

Christianity was something extremely vital to Charles Tindley. Whenever he preached, he preached to win. Seldom did he conclude a service without extending an altar call.

During a memorable invitation, a bleary-eyed white man made his way forward. Soon Tindley was kneeling by his side and praying with him. Minutes later, the two were on their feet, their arms locked in mutual embrace. Then, his voice a trifle husky, Dr. Tindley said, "Friends, I want you to know this young man who has just given his heart to God. He is the grandson of the Maryland planter who once owned me as a slave!"

With a crowded church, adequate finances, and a vigorous program of evangelism going on, Tindley could have relaxed. In the eyes of the world, he had arrived. But he had earlier resolved to be as effective as possible; so now he learned New Testament Greek through correspondence.

But New Testament Greek was not enough for Charles

Tindley; he also had to learn Hebrew! A friendly rabbi agreed to tutor him in this difficult language so that he could read the Old Testament in the original. He neglected nothing that could produce extra spiritual vitamins for his people.

One evening, Tindley was writing his Sunday morning sermon when suddenly there was a dark shadow across the page. Quick examination showed that a puff of wind had blown a piece of paper through the window and that the paper had settled between the oil lamp and his manuscript. He removed the paper and then began to mentally make a spiritual application. Soon the sermon was neglected as he found himself writing a hymn—a hymn that was to inspire millions. Titled, "Nothing Between," here is the first verse:

> Nothing between my soul and the Savior
> Naught of this world's delusive dream;
> I have renounced all sinful pleasure,
> Jesus is mine; let nothing between.

Goading himself to do more and more for the Lord, he made a practice of rising at 4 a.m. Those early hours were spent in prayer and study. There were few religious books that did not come under his eyes. At the time of his passing, he owned eight thousand books, yet his main book was the Bible.

During the depression, Tindley inspired his church to help the needy; many a family retained its dignity because of him. When the mayor came to investigate this side of his work, he was so impressed he gave him a personal check for $3,000.

Visitors were constantly dropping into church to learn the secret of his power. When questioned, one of his twelve children replied that his father had attained his success on his knees. But there was also a human aspect— an aspect that was honed and polished by the Holy Spirit. He had a unique way of relating to people and directing their spiritual needs to the correct source of supply.

For many weeks a lady continued to come to his study with the same burden. He was always glad to listen; but in time he tired of hearing the same thing. Finally, in exasperation, he exclaimed, "Why don't you take your burden to the Lord and leave it there?"

Inspired by this impromptu statement, he wrote a hymn which he named, "Leave It There." The first verse of that still-popular number went straight to the heart of the problem:

> If the world from you withhold of its silver and its gold,
> And you have to get along on meager fare,
> Just remember, from on high He will every need supply;
> Take your burden to the Lord and leave it there.*

Thinking over this remarkable man's life, one wonders when he experienced his finest hour. There were banquets in his honor; offers of a bishopric; honorary degrees; and innumerable special recognitions. But perhaps his greatest hour came when he was pastor of the tiny church at Cape May.

At the time, he was poverty stricken. Tindley's need was increased one winter by a blizzard that howled through the city. Nothing edible was in the house but some stale bread, which the family dipped in water and fed to the two surviving children. Their baby daughter had died in the cold the night before, and there wasn't a single cent for burial.

At breakfast time Tindley insisted that his wife set the table.

"But there is nothing to eat!" she complained.

"Never mind. Just set it as you usually do."

Then facing the empty plates, Tindley knelt with his wife at the customary place. In his prayer that morning, he

*Copyright by Hope Publishing Co. Used by permission.

thanked the Lord for his good health, the opportunity to serve, the joy of salvation, and for his children.

Suddenly their prayers were interrupted by a knock at the door. And there in the midst of the storm stood a white man, the ear flaps of his cap down. His arms were loaded with groceries. "I'm sorry I'm a little late," he apologized. "But the snow's been pretty heavy."

It was a hard test. But Charles Tindley passed with his flags at full-mast and snapping in the breeze.

2

The Martyr of Prague

Slowly, methodically, the executioners removed the victim's outer garments. Next, they tied his hands behind his back and bound him with seven water-soaked ropes to the short, thick stake.

Because of the excitement, they did not at first notice that the man who was to be burned was facing the east. When their mistake was discovered, they immediately twisted the body until it faced the west. This was the proper position for heretics, and a heretic as notorious as John Hus should not have special favors!

A rusty chain was now thrown around his neck and locked to the back of the stake. This was to keep the body from slumping after the ropes had charred through. While this was being done, John Hus commented in a rather toneless voice, "My Lord Jesus was for my sake bound with one much heavier; why should I, poor wretch, not let myself be bound with this for His holy name's sake?"

Bundles of dry faggots were now mixed with straw and pushed around his feet. Then the straw was piled around him until it reached his chin.

The torch that would fire the combustibles sputtered and shivered nearby. Instinctively the eyes of Hus, and those of the enormous crowd overflowing the meadow, focused on the orange-yellow flame that would soon be ending a life.

Von Pappenheim, Marshal of the Empire, now went over to him; in the name of the king he demanded that Hus recant. If only he would change his mind about his doctrines, his life would be saved. Just one word—a single word—and he would be removed from the stake, and perhaps even be given his freedom.

Hus wasn't tempted. "What heresies should I recant when I am not aware of a single one? I call God to witness that I have neither taught nor preached what false witnesses have charged me with. The foremost aim of all my deeds and writings was to turn men from sin . . . and in this truth I will gladly die!"

As he finished, von Pappenheim gave a shrug and galloped off. Then the grim-faced officer who represented legal authority reached for the torch. While the crowd waited for the blaze to ignite, thoughts and memories seared through every mind.

There were some who had come to Constance on that warm July 6, 1415, because they made a habit of going to executions. Watching others die made them feel less guilty of their own sins. But there were many others among the milling thousands who had followed the career of John Hus very closely. Some of them knew the main details from the time of his birth; a few—a very few—were sympathetic with him. His main source of friends was Bohemia, scores of miles away. The sympathetic ones prayed silently that he would withstand the trial. Many felt this might be a turning point in history.

John Hus was born in 1373 in Husinecz, a village in southern Bohemia, to a poor family. His father died when John was a small boy, but his mother tried to make up for the father's care by lavishing affection on him. She took him to school and went with him to Prague where he enrolled in its famous university in 1389.

Without family resources, John was extremely poor and was forced to supply a part of his support by singing in various churches and even on the streets. But his passion for education was deeper than his poverty, and he sometimes went without food while earning a B.A., B.D., and M.A. He was ordained to the priesthood in 1401.

His sense of piety was a keen one. Longing for holiness, he purchased a certificate of pardon at Wyssehrad for four pennies—the last money he had.

In 1402 he became pastor of Prague's preaching center, Bethlehem Chapel. Preaching in his native Czech, and fearlessly denouncing everything he felt wrong, he soon attracted vast throngs. He was not afraid of the clergy or the hierarchy of the church even though he knew they could destroy him. Speaking before the Synod in Prague, he was so pointed his hearers gasped.

Jabbing with his finger as he denounced hireling ministers, he thundered: "Such ministers speak evil in high places, calling out that all who disobey them are heretics and that they have the power to condemn to hell . . . These hireling priests are wolves preying on the flock and are of antichrist the great wolf. . . . They are now so many in number and so influential that they seize faithful shepherds who feed their flocks on the pastures of God's Word, and put them to death as heretics."

The writings of John Wycliffe, known as "The Morning Star of the Reformation," had already been making an impact on Bohemia for twenty years. Protected from the pope by the English throne, his tongue and pen sizzled with the wrath of his pronouncements.

Attacking transubstantiation—the doctrine proclaiming the presence of Christ in the Eucharist—he wrote in the English of his day: it is "grounded nether in Holy Writt ne reson ne wit but only taughte by new hypocritis and cursed heretikis that magnyfyen there own fantasies and dremes."

He also wrote against indulgences and ridiculed the idea that the Roman church was supreme above all churches. These ideas took such root in the university at Prague that many debates were staged over them, and the faculty became divided. The teachings of Wycliffe became so controversial the university called a council and by majority vote decreed that they should never be taught either privately or in public.

At first Hus paid little attention to Wycliffe's writings. His discipleship to Wycliffe was fostered by others. A common saying in Prague declared: "Wycliffe begat Stanislaus of Znaim, Stanislaus of Znaim begat Peter of Znaim; Peter of Znaim begat Palecz, and Palecz begat Hus."

But when Hus did start reading Wycliffe, he became attracted to him as a moth is attracted to a light. Soon he began to write books of his own—books that contained long quotations from Wycliffe. Moreover, his denunciations of the clergy in his sermons at Bethlehem Chapel became even more caustic.

A bull from the pope reached Prague in 1410. In this document, the pontiff decreed that all of Wycliffe's books were to be burned, and that preaching services could only be conducted at certain specified points. All persons possessing Wycliffe's books were to turn them in for burning. Any who refused to do this within six days were to be excommunicated—and no one would be allowed to eat or trade or even to speak with them. It was a drastic measure.

About two hundred books were burned in the court of

the archbishop's palace on July 16, 1410. A Te Deum was sung while the flames lapped up the books—many in beautiful and expensive bindings.

The fire frightened a large section of Wycliffe's followers into silence. Hus, however, was incensed. Within days he was on a public platform defending some of Wycliffe's doctrines, and arguing that it is wrong to destroy books even though they contain heresies. He bolstered his logic with quotations from Jerome, Augustine and Ambrose.

From this point on, Hus grew bolder in his writings and condemnation of the church hierarchy. And every day the breach between himself and the pope widened. He wrote tract after tract upholding the doctrines of Wycliffe and denouncing the pope.

In 1412, some of the clergy in Prague wrote to the pope and demanded that Hus be punished to the full extent of the law. Their letter insisted that "every heretic and schismatic deserves a place with the devil and his angels in the flames of eternal fire."

As things worsened, it was decided that Hus should present his case to the Council at Constance—a meeting at which most of the powers of Europe would be represented. Friends advised him not to go, insisting that he would be arrested, and that he would never come back. Emperor Sigismund, however, assured him that he would be safe; and so, with this assurance, he left Prague on October 14th.

Hus arrived in Constance on Sunday, November 3. He secured a room in the house of the widow Fida, and there waited for the proceedings to start. While he waited, Constance filled with celebrities. Among these were 33 cardinals, 47 archbishops, and 217 doctors of theology. Representatives came from 37 universities, and there were 83 envoys representing various kings.

The celebrities did not come alone; each one felt compelled to bring along a train of servants. John of

Nassau, the archbishop of Mainz, was accompanied by seven hundred horsemen. Constance witnessed medieval pageantry at its peak. The city of six thousand was suddenly overflowing with one hundred thousand.

Hus, however, could not enjoy the gala occasion; within a few days of his arrival, he was arrested and thrown into prison. The guarantee of safety was a cruel joke.

On July 6 he faced his judges at the cathedral in Constance. King Sigismund sat on a raised throne in full vestments, and at his feet were the robed dignitaries of the Empire. The session started with a Mass, and then the Bishop of Lodi preached on Romans 6: 6. He emphasized the portion of the text concerning the destruction of the body of sin. The sermon was directed at Hus.

Next, the charges were read—most of which were utterly fantastic. But each charge was considered accurate because it concluded with the words: "Proven by a doctor of theology," or "Proven by a priest."

One charge declared that Hus had considered himself to be a fourth member of the Trinity. "Tell me the name of the doctor who witnessed this against me," begged Hus.

"That is not necessary," replied the reader coldly.

Hus felt his stomach churn within. But he could do nothing, nor could anyone else; for it had been decreed that anyone who caused a disturbance would be excommunicated and imprisoned for two months!

Suddenly John Hus was so outraged he reminded the emperor that he had been guaranteed safe conduct both to and from the council.

History records that when he did this, Sigismund blushed scarlet.

After the death sentence had been pronounced, Hus was forced to don his priestly robes. The communion chalice was then thrust into his hand.

Next, his robes were removed by the bishops and the cup was taken away. While this was being done, the leader pronounced the following curse: "Damned Judas, as you left the council of peace and made one with the Jews, lo, we take away from you the chalice of salvation."

Next, his hair was cut crosswise so that it would not resemble the tonsure of a priest. Then an eighteen-inch paper cap with three devils painted on it was clamped on his head. This being done, he was led to the courtyard where his books were being burned.

Then he was taken to a stake at the city outskirts.

Presently the man with the torch touched the straw at the feet of his victim. As the flames rose, Hus prayed out loud, "Oh, God, have mercy on me." Then in a clear, loud voice, he sang: "Jesus Christ, Son of the living God, have mercy on me." He repeated this a second time, and started to repeat it a third time. But a puff of wind blew a flame into his face, thus silencing him.

His bones were then ground into bits and tossed into the nearby Rhine. His garments were also burned, for the judges did not want any souvenirs taken back to Bohemia.

But that night, while the crowd was busy with various entertainments, followers of Hus slipped out to the stake and gathered handfuls of earth. The soil was then sent back to Prague. There it was greeted with tears—and determination.

3

Old Rugged Cross

The young tenor's debut was a smashing success. The crowd clapped for one encore after another. The singer had hoped for three or four encores, and had practiced for them—but this crowd clapped and shouted for a sixth! What was he to do?

"Go back! You must sing something!" insisted the teacher from the wing.

"But—but what?" demanded the pale-faced youth. "I'm not prepared!"

"Maybe—maybe you could sing something you've sung in church."

Wondering if this was the correct thing to do on such an occasion, he returned to the microphone and began to sing "The Old Rugged Cross."

Immediately a stillness came over the people. But when he concluded there was neither stamping nor shouting. Instead, men and women all over the auditorium began to reach for their handkerchiefs.

The story of the Cross had reached their hearts!

But this triumph was nothing new for the famous hymn. Such effects on the listener occurred with almost monotonous regularity. When she returned to China, the missionary Alice Shaefer took along some phonograph records. One day while she was playing them at the Ming Sam School for the blind in Canton, a little blind girl, who was afflicted with a disorder causing temper tantrums, suddenly became quiet when "The Old Rugged Cross" was played.

Puzzled by this extraordinary phenomenon, Miss Shaefer had a phonograph ready to play the records should the girl have another tantrum. And it worked—immediately! The girl could not understand the words, but the rhythm or melody had a soothing effect on her.

Since its first publication in 1913, "The Old Rugged Cross" has sold millions of copies and has continued as a favorite. In 1938 NBC polled its listeners to discover the two most popular songs. Somewhat to the amazement of the executives, "The Old Rugged Cross" was voted the number-one favorite.

In 1931 the famous hymn was dropped from the Methodist Hymnal, but in 1966 it was returned to the hymnal with an initial print order of over two million!

George Bennard was born on a cold February 4, 1873, in Youngstown, Ohio. Sometime after this, the family moved to Albia, Iowa, where the father earned a meager living in the mines. Things were going reasonably well for the family when a pile of slate worked loose and fell on the father. He never recovered.

Following this disaster, the responsibility of earning a living was pushed onto the shoulders of 16-year-old George. Having a mother and four sisters to support, he went into the mines and worked like a man.

In 1895 he was converted at a Salvation Army meeting. Promoted three years later to Adjutant, he led a traveling Army brigade on evangelistic trips throughout the Midwest. Later, he was sent to New York where he remained with the Salvationists until 1910. He then struck out on his own, conducting revivals and writing hymns.

From this period, we have several lesser known compositions. These include: "Speak, My Lord!" "Oh, Make Me Clean," and "Have Thy Way, Lord."

The idea of "The Old Rugged Cross" did not come until a time of great anxiety and frustration in 1913. "I was praying," he remembered, "for a full understanding of the Cross. . . . While watching this scene, the theme came to me and along with it the melody."

Where the hymn was actually written is a point of debate. Several cities claim the honor. The reason for the uncertainty is because Bennard was on the road at the time, speaking night after night in various churches. Fortunately we have his own word: "At the time I was traveling with a Salvation Army brigade, and I'd write a part of a verse and a few bars of music at a time, fitting the lyric to the melody as I went along. Then, when I had the melody pretty well in mind, I would either put the notes for that part of the score on paper, or have someone else do it for me as I hummed the tune.

"I finished both the melody and the lyric one night in Albion, Michigan."

The writing of the hymn and melody took about one month.

A special memorial was erected in honor of Bennard at Pokagon, Michigan—a heavy rugged cross standing behind a granite boulder with the following inscription carved in the stone:

" 'The Old Rugged Cross,' composed by George Bennard, was first sung in this church by a choir composed of Frank Virgil, Olive Marrs, Clara Virgil, William Thaldorf.

Florence Jones, organist. Arthur Dodd, violinist."

The old Methodist church building where the choir had first sung the hymn is no longer in use, but Frank Virgil, a member of the first choir to sing the hymn, remembers the event.

"Reverend Bennard was conducting revival services in our church," explained Virgil. "The meeting was planned for two weeks, but because of increased interest it went on for another week.

"The evangelist stayed with our minister, L. O. Bostwick. Early one morning I took some groceries over to the parsonage. While I was watching Mrs. Bostwick fry some side pork in the kitchen, Bennard came in with his guitar. 'I want to play you a new hymn I have written,' he said.

"Bennard then sang 'The Old Rugged Cross,' accompanying himself on the guitar.

" 'How does it sound?' he said, after he had finished.

" 'It will go far,' she said.

"I'll never forget that day. It was a great moment. I, too, was convinced that I had heard a great hymn."

The hymn became popular immediately. It was brought out in published form by the Homer Rodeheaver Company and copyrighted by them. Radio, in those days, was just in its beginnings; nevertheless, radio helped spread the hymn across the country and later, around the world.

On October 27, 1929, The Women's Foreign Missionary Society of the Methodist Church gathered in Memorial Hall in Columbus, Ohio, to celebrate their 60th anniversary. Homer Rodeheaver, song leader for the occasion, had arranged for Mario Capelli, the noted Italian-American singer, to be the guest artist.

While Capelli was singing, "I will cling to the old rugged cross," he threw his arms around a huge cross on the platform. Later, he confessed, "I never knew the significance of the Cross until that night."

Because of the fame of his hymn, Bennard was able to

preach the Gospel in many new places. During Billy Graham's early ministry, he proudly introduced Bennard to a revival crowd, explaining that he was the author of "The Old Rugged Cross." After the service, an elderly lady shook his hand while she exclaimed, "Well, I'm glad to meet the one who wrote 'The Old Oaken Bucket.'"

Bennard, of course, was proud the Lord had enabled him to write the famous song. His greatest satisfaction, however, was not from the three hundred fifty hymns which he had written. "When I pass," he used to say. "I would rather be remembered as a preacher of the Gospel than as a maker of music, which to me is secondary to the spreading of the Lord's Word."

In later years he moved to a farm five miles north of Reed City, Michigan. While there, at age 85, he passed away during an asthma attack.

The Reed City Chamber of Commerce has created the Old Rugged Cross Park in his honor. And close by his home they erected a huge cross. The cross and park are visited by thousands each year.

4

End of a Feud

No one knows exactly why the Hatfield-McCoy feud started, but nearly everyone knows that it smoked and bubbled like a cauldron for more than 25 years, and that it bloodied many a hill in Kentucky and West Virginia.

The courts did their best to silence the sharpshooters. They handed down stiff jail sentences and sprang the trap on many gallows, but the feudists ignored the law completely. Then a mountain preacher became concerned about Devil Anse, leader of the Hatfields. He quoted the Word, and there were tears and confessions. Soon he pulled in the net and a few days later Devil Anse plus two of the boys were baptized in the Main Island Creek.

This act of faith and obedience muzzled the guns, and soon the Hatfields and McCoys were shaking hands, running for public office, and living decent lives. The feud had been settled by the Gospel!

The Tug Fork flows between West Virginia and Kentucky, later becoming part of the Big Sandy. The stream forms an excellent border between the two states for many miles. But unfortunately that same stream seemed to emphasize the differences between the Kentucky McCoys and the West Virginia Hatfields. This is mountain country, where traces of Elizabethan English linger and where a six-gun stood next to baby's cradle. It used to be a land where people's memories seethed over past grievances, and where grudges were willed from one generation to the next.

William Anderson Hatfield, commonly called Devil Anse, was a six-footer with a dark shovel-beard, gray eyes, sloping shoulders, the cunning of a fox, and the memory of an elephant. He could not distinguish one letter from another, but he could speed a bullet in the direction he wanted it to go. Sometimes he stood on the bank of the Tug Fork and clipped the necks from bottles as they floated by. He did this for practice—and he did it without raising his guns above his waist.

Devil Anse erected his cabin near the mouth of Peter Creek, close to the place where it joins the Tug. He had 12 children, each instructed in the sins of the McCoys—especially those of Randolph McCoy and his brood.

Randolph McCoy was twenty years older than Devil Anse, but the two men were very similar. McCoy also had a formidable memory. But unlike Devil Anse, he was not given to pranks and his lips seldom parted in a smile.

McCoy's cabin was at Turkeyfoot on the slope of a Kentucky mountain, where he brooded with his wife and 13 children. The homes of the antagonists were a mere seven or eight miles apart.

The Hatfields and McCoys fought each other during the Civil War, but this fighting was merely because they had different ideals and different flags. The first trouble didn't start until about 1873, and that was started by a razor-back hog.

In those days pigs were not always fenced in. Instead,

they were identified by notches in their ears. One day Floyd Hatfield, a cousin of Devil Anse, herded a group of pigs across the Tug into Kentucky and locked them in a pen near Stringtown. Two days later Randolph McCoy galloped up to the pigsty. His keen eyes studied the pigs for a while, and then he snapped, "Floyd, that ain't yo' hawg."

Floyd was a little shocked, for he and McCoy had married sisters.

"Yes, it is," he said warmly. "That notch in his ear is mine. I remember when I done cut it."

"No, it ain't!" contradicted McCoy.

"Yes, it is," returned Hatfield, his face crimson.

Finally it was decided to take the matter to court. The court was presided over by Rev. Anderson Hatfield, a Baptist preacher from Raccoon Hollow and a cousin of Devil Anse. The day of the trial the preacher's cabin was jammed with relatives from both sides. The smell of snuff and liquor mingled with the smell of Exhibit A—the pig.

With glowering Hatfields on one side and tense McCoys on the other, the preacher faced a problem—a problem that could silence him in the entire mountain area. Praying for the dexterity of Solomon, he appointed a jury composed of six McCoys and six Hatfields.

As the witnesses shuffled forward to testify, it became evident that the slant of the testimony depended upon the clan to which the witness belonged. The strongest evidence was offered by Bill Staton. Under oath, he declared that he had seen Floyd notch the pig's ears with his very own eyes. The McCoys accused him of lying on behalf of the Hatfields because he was related to them by marriage.

The arguments finished, the preacher polled the jury—asking them one by one for their opinion. The jury would have been deadlocked except for the testimony of Selkirk McCoy. After a nervous cough, he said he believed the pig belonged to Floyd Hatfield. This bold statement infuriated the McCoys. They dubbed him a traitor, and blamed his stand on the influence of his wife—a Hatfield.

Hatfield got his pig, but the controversy continued. As the mountaineers argued the case, punctuating their words with amber tobacco juice, the merits and demerits of the case began to harden into dark hatreds.

Within hours, Randolph McCoy confronted Staton and during a tongue lashing called him a liar. Then he heaved a stone at him. The bitterness increased on both sides. Violence did not break out at once. Nevertheless, the fuse had been lit. The community was alarmed, for the pious elders knew that things were about to blow.

But nothing serious happened until 1880, when Bill Staton and his brother John poled a flat-bottom up the Tug Fork. Suddenly from around the curve, another boat appeared carrying Floyd McCoy and his brother Calvin. The two sets of men glared at each other and then their guns began to boom. But even though they were normally crack shots, no one was even scratched.

Then Bill Staton disappeared. The search party found him sprawled near his gun. The hole in his head and the crushed foliage pointed to foul play. The mountains hummed with the story. Soon it was noticed that both Paris and Sam McCoy—nephews of Randolph McCoy— had vanished. This was strong evidence, and the evidence increased when Paris returned with a bullet wound in his hip.

Suspicions alerted, the Hatfields went on a search and soon came back with Sam McCoy. Next, Ellison Hatfield, a brother of Devil Anse and the husband of Bill Staton's sister, swore out a warrant for the McCoys' arrests. But the verdict of the court was that Sam and Paris had been shot in self-defense, and so they were freed.

This action blew the slumbering coals of hatred into a blaze that was to roar through the mountains for years. The McCoys had Devil Anse's son Johnse indicted for selling moonshine in Kentucky. Randolph McCoy's son Tolbert got himself deputized and arrested Johnse. But Devil Anse caught up with them and released the prisoner. And so the quarrel blazed like a forest fire. Then the press took it up. A headline on the Hatfield-McCoy feud was bound to sell newspapers.

Again and again a Hatfield or a McCoy was ambushed, and he perished with a bullet in his heart. And again and again the newsboys in Boston and New York shouted, "Hatfield-McCoy feud revived. Read all about it." Truth got mingled with fiction, and the feud that cost from thirty to two hundred lives became a focal point of interest, inspiring plays and motion pictures.

The mention of the feud often brought a smile; but William Dyke Garrett, a Baptist preacher from the mountains, never saw any humor in it. He had marched with Devil Anse during the Civil War. Now he began to direct his prayers at Devil Anse and occasionally stopped in to see him. At such times he always poked in a word for the Lord.

Around 1910, Elias and Troy, sons of Devil Anse, opened a saloon in Boomer. In a cold-blooded deal with another liquor-man, they divided up the town. Each one agreed to stay out of the other's territory. The other man, however, didn't keep the agreement. In flagrant violation of the contract, he sent an Italian out to peddle moonshine in Hatfield territory. The brothers went to see the Italian, to warn him away. Elias approached the front door and Troy the rear. But their competitor was ready. Elias was stopped with a bullet in his heart, and Troy with a bullet in his bowels. But before Troy died he managed to put a bullet in the Italian's heart, another in his brain, and another in his stomach. Thus in moments, all three died.

This was the first time immediate members of Devil Anse's family had been killed, and he was shaken. Indeed, he was so shaken he called on Uncle Dyke.

The preacher had been praying and was ready for his caller. Skillfully he shifted the conversation to the story of the Cross, the Resurrection, the Atonement, and he emphasized the "whosoever" of the New Testament. This time Devil Anse was ready.

The coming baptism of the leader of the Hatfields drew a large crowd; and on that Sunday as he and his sons disappeared beneath the water for a moment, the amazed crowd knew that they had really been converted. The feud had come to an end. Devil Anse still had his guns and he could still shoot straight. Sitting on his porch, he faced a swaying can on a string about thirty yards away. Suddenly he picked up his rifle and without putting his eye to the sights, he pulled the trigger four times. When the can was retrieved they found it had four holes in it.

Devil Anse lived the Christian life until his death in 1921. Uncle Dyke took care of the final services. After the service, the procession wound its way up to the mountain cemetery just above the church. Then, while an umbrella was opened to protect the oak casket, the lid was raised for a last look.

As the viewers gazed again at the shovel-beard, now tinged with gray, and the hooked nose, they did so with deep respect. And among those who found it hard to swallow were a number of McCoys.

Old Devil Anse had had the courage to confess Christ, to change his ways, to be an example to the community. And everyone appreciated it.

5

The Salvation of the Old Blasphemer

Few hymns have remained as popular as "Amazing Grace." And without a doubt the main reason is that John Newton wrote from personal experience. Like the hymn, his incredible story is that of grace—Amazing Grace. Today, as church buildings fill with the enthusiastic harmony of the hymn, it is almost impossible to realize that the author was once a deserter, a blasphemer, a drunk, and a slaver. Nevertheless, we have the facts!

The hymn, and especially the following verse, is a thumbnail biography of his checkered beginnings:

Through many dangers, toils, and snares,
   I have already come;
'Tis grace hath brought me safe thus far,
   And grace will lead me home.

John Newton was born on July 24, 1725. His well-to-do father commanded a ship that traded in the Mediterranean. John and his mother were very close, and she [took] special interest in giving him an early education. B[y the] time he was four he could read and at six he was stud[ying] Latin.

His mother died when he was only seven, and since his father was often gone on long voyages, he felt the loss acutely. Shortly after this tragedy, the father remarried and John was exiled to a boarding school in Essex.

His brilliant brain absorbed knowledge like a sponge. Soon the astonished teachers were pushing him as fast as he could go. He later thought they pushed him too fast; before he was 10 he was reading Virgil in Latin.

Soon his father decided that he had been in school long enough and that he should start learning the secrets of the sea. So at the age of 11, John Newton climbed the gangplank onto the first ship where he was employed. In the ship's library he found many Christian books which he began to read. But he also heard the purple oaths of the sailors; since oaths seemed more attractive than tedious books of sermons, he decided to become a champion blasphemer. Thus, whenever his father was at a distance, he colored the air with the most dreadful language he could dredge from his fertile brain.

A year after his initial voyage, he was thrown from a horse and landed a few inches from a freshly-cut hedgerow. The murderous stakes were extremely sharp. This narrow escape turned him again toward the New Testament. He even began to pray. But at this time his religious enthusiasms never lasted. Then followed a period of wild, shameful sinning. Convicted again, he began to pray and go on long fasts. Concerning this period, he wrote: "I became an ascetic, and endeavored, so far as my situation would permit, to renounce society, that I might avoid temptation. I continued in this serious mood (I cannot give it a higher title) for more than two years without a considerable breaking off. It left me, in many respects, er the power of sin."

At 16 he met 13-year-old Mary Catlett in Kent and fell deeply in love with her. From then on, his heart and mind remained in Kent, and every spare moment between voyages was spent with her.

The elder Newton became so discouraged with John he arranged for him to join the British Navy where, he hoped, he would acquire some discipline. Signing as a midshipman, the lad took a berth on the *Harwich,* a well known man-of-war.

During his first month in the navy he met and idolized a free-thinker who turned him even farther from God and led him into deeper sin. Then by mere chance, the new friend sailed on another ship. The vessel was caught in a violent storm on the way to Lisbon and a wave swept him to his death.

That December, while the *Harwich* was at port in Plymouth, John learned that his father had made a connection with an African company. Longing to join him, he decided to jump ship at the first opportunity. The opportunity came sooner than he had hoped. Ordered ashore to make certain no one deserted, he deserted himself. Two days later he was arrested and marched back to the ship in irons. Then, following 48 hours in the brig, he was publicly flogged. In addition, he lost his rank.

The sailors on the ship refused to speak to him. In agony because of this and because of his loss of rank, he was tempted to commit suicide. But a strange impulse restrained him.

Some time later, John Newton obtained a discharge from the *Harwich* and joined a slaver headed for Sierra Leone. It turned out that the captain knew his father. But ignoring this, John decided to "let himself go." He swore with such fluency even the hardened sailors were ashamed of him. And when the captain displeased him, he composed a song that ridiculed him, the ship, and even his motives. Then he taught it to everyone on board!

After numerous voyages on other ships to Africa, John Newton found himself accused of dishonesty. Indeed, things became so intolerable for him, he asked permission to stay in Africa with the "factor"—the one whose job it was to have the slaves ready for shipment.

It turned out that this factor had a seething hatred of John Newton. When Newton succumbed to a fever, he and his wife collaborated in making him miserable. She alternately starved him and then allowed him scraps from her own plate. Had it not been that he caught an occasional fish, he would have starved. "If I saw a fish upon my hook my joy was little less than any other person may have found in the accomplishment of the scheme he had most at heart. Such a fish, hastily broiled, or rather, half burned, without sauce, salt, or bread, afforded me a delicious meal."

He was also forced to live in the open. "The rainy season was now advancing. My clothing was a shirt, a pair of trousers, a cotton handkerchief, instead of a cap, and a cotton cloth about two yards long for upper garments." In this condition, "I have been exposed for twenty, thirty, perhaps nearly forty hours together in incessant rains accompanied with strong gales of wind . . ."

His life at this time was worse than that of an animal. And so what did he do to occupy his mind? He measured out space on the sand and mastered the first six books of Euclid! Thus geometry kept him from going insane.

Upon recovering from the fever that nearly took his life, he saw a ship skirting the shore. The captain was obviously looking for trade and so Newton made a smoke signal. The ship responded and Newton was picked up. At first he was so thankful for being rescued he behaved himself. But soon he began to drink heavily, blaspheme, and cause trouble. Then the ship was caught in a dreadful storm.

"But now the Lord's time was come, and the conviction

that I was so unwilling to receive was deeply impressed on me. I went to bed that night in my usual security and indifference but was awakened from a sound sleep by the force of the violent sea, which broke on us. Much of it came down below and filled the cabin where I lay with water. This alarm was followed by a cry that the ship was going down. . . . As soon as I could recover myself, I started to go on deck, but was met on the ladder by the captain, who desired me to bring a knife . . . .

"While returning with the knife, another person went up in my place, who was instantly washed overboard . . . . The sea had torn away the upper timbers on one side, and made the ship a mere wreck. . . ."

Newton and others went to the pumps, but the water came in faster than they could pump it out. Had it not been that they were loaded with timber and beeswax, they would have sunk. The sailors labored all night and used their clothes to stuff up the leaks. By dawn they began to win the battle and Newton began to pray. Deeply troubled, he went to his New Testament and was especially comforted by John 7: 17: "If any man will do his will, he shall know of the doctrine, whether it be of God, or whether I speak of myself." Newton, then and there, determined to do the will of God. But in his heart he knew he was not really saved.

The storm had done terrible damage. All the livestock had been swept into the sea; and the only food left was some fish and some garbage intended for the hogs. Most of the sails had been blown away and there were barely enough to keep them moving.

The weather calmed. Still the ship was in great peril. "We had incessant labor with the pumps, to keep the ship above water. Much labor and little food wasted us fast, and one man died. Yet our sufferings were light in comparison to our fears. We had a terrible prospect of being either starved to death or reduced to feed on each other.

Our expectations grew darker every day."

During this time of peril, the captain grew morose and sarcastic. He also developed a special loathing for John Newton. He called him a Jonah, and blamed his troubles on him and kept mumbling that he should be thrown overboard.

Finally, a month from the time of the wreck, the ship anchored at Lough Swilly in Ireland. And it was about this time that Newton felt that his prayers were being heard. He pored over his New Testament—lingering especially with such parables as that of the Prodigal Son. Then on shore, he began to attend church services. After almost unbelievable anxiety, he felt assurance of his salvation.

Then on February 1, 1750, he journeyed to Kent and married his childhood sweetheart, Mary Catlett. They set up a home and he continued to earn his living at sea. Working hard, he soon became the captain of a ship engaged in the slave trade. That he could profess to be an evangelical Christian and at the same time remain a slaver seems an impossibility. But in his day, slavery was not considered an evil; indeed, many Christians invested in the business.

On these voyages, Newton mastered Greek and Hebrew and soon began to feel his call to the ministry. At first the bishops refused to even consider him. But after a while, when he insisted that God had called him, and he demonstrated his understanding of the Bible, he was duly ordained.

Most of John Newton's ministry was spent at Olney where he constantly preached to a crowded church. Feeling that the masses could grasp the Gospel better if it were presented in simple hymns, he joined with his friend William Cowper in writing a hymnal. It was for this hymnal that Newton wrote "Amazing Grace" and "How Sweet the Name of Jesus Sounds."

As Newton matured spiritually, he saw the enormous

evil of slavery. He wrote and spoke against it and became one of its most bitter opponents. Indeed, he provided much of the fire that inspired William Wilberforce to fight it in the House of Commons until it was finally abolished in the British Empire.

His perpetual sweetheart Mary died in 1790. But he continued on for another 17 years. He knew that his sins had been forgiven; but his days as a slaver continued to haunt him. When writing to special friends, he often signed his name: The Old African Blasphemer.

At 80, he was plagued with poor health and failing vision. When friends urged that he retire, he exclaimed: "What! Shall the Old African Blasphemer stop when he can yet speak?"

On the Wednesday before his death, someone inquired about his faith. Newton replied immediately: "I am satisfied with the Lord's will."

His final summons came on December 21, 1807. He was 82.

The calmness of the tamed giant as he neared the gates reminded many of his famous hymn:

> Amazing grace! (how sweet the sound!)
>   That saved a wretch like me;
> I once was lost, but now am found;
>   Was blind, but now I see.

6

The Secrets of the Pole

As the fierce Antarctic winds snarled about his tent, Captain Robert Falcon Scott knew that he and his three companions would soon freeze to death. The last nibble of food had been swallowed. And although there was a large supply of pemmican and other edibles in a food depot only 11 miles away, he knew it was impossible to get to it. Eleven miles now was as remote as a thousand or a million.

Fearing that Scott and his men might come to such an end, those who had prepared this 1910 expedition to the South Pole had sent along a supply of opium. A dose would send the trapped men into a land of pleasant dreams and they would not fear the terrors of the cold. Now death was rattling the frozen flaps of their tent; but instead of reaching for opium, Scott fumbled for his pen and paper in order to write and address letters he trusted would reach his friends, his wife, and small son Peter.

With a calmness that amazed the world, he wrote until his fingers were too numb to hold a pen. One of these fantastic letters was addressed to an old friend, Sir James Barrie. "We are in a desperate state, feet frozen, etc. No fuel and a long way from food, but it would do your heart good to be in our tent and to hear our songs and cheery conversation. . . ."

During those last tragic hours, Scott and his companions felt the strength that comes to those who "trust in the everlasting arms." Evidence of this is shown in the letters found eight months later, tucked in notebooks wedged beneath his frozen shoulders. Today this daring man has become a symbol of courage to the world. The diaries of his last heroic mission are still intact.

The Antarctic has intrigued men ever since its mainland was discovered by Captain Nathaniel Brown Palmer, an American searching for seals in 1820. Since then, in spite of winds that frequently blow at 200 miles an hour, and of temperatures that sag to 125 degrees below zero, the nations of the world have sought to explore its treasures.

From the time Scott became a naval cadet at the age of 13, he dreamed of visiting Antarctica. And sometimes when his dreams really got wild, he imagined being the first one to reach the South Pole.

As his father watched during this period, he shook his head and dubbed Robert "old mooney." But Scott knotted his dreams with work. By the time he was 20 he had passed the stiff examinations with honors, and was made a sublieutenant.

He could have been content with his position in the British Navy. It had security and offered steady advancement, but his vision and energy would not allow this. He dug into every book he could find to learn more about those areas beyond the mysterious frozen Circle. He was determined that someday he was going to sail there and explore that difficult land.

This interest came to the attention of others. By the time Scott was 31 he was chosen to lead the First British Expedition to explore the practically unknown Antarctica Continent—a continent two-thirds the size of North America. Sailing from England in 1900, he led the party to the land of his boyhood dreams.

Scott's ship, *Discovery,* returned to England on September 10, 1904. Scott was given a hero's welcome and was promoted to captain. These honors were deserved, for he and his party in spite of almost incredible difficulties, had explored Victoria Mountains; the Ross Ice Barrier; and had discovered and named King Edward Island.

Enthusiasm for the ice-capped land to the south that bottomed the world like a saucer continued to spread, and that enthusiasm overpowered Scott. In 1909 he announced that he was organizing a second expedition. And on June 1, 1910, he sailed the *Terra Nova* down the Thames on the first part of his new journey to the Pole.

With great confidence, he headed toward McMurdo Sound where he intended to establish a base and a string of supply depots stretching toward the Pole.

The men were optimistic—perhaps too optimistic. On Christmas Day they crowded into a room on the ship where services were being held, honored Christ, and thanked Him for the success they were experiencing.

The *Terra Nova* was duly anchored at McMurdo Sound on January 3, 1911. And then the work of building a solid base began. Scott wrote in his diary with appreciation for his men. "Thursday, January 5. All hands were up at 5:00 this morning. Words cannot express the splendid way in which everyone works and gradually the work gets organized. I was a little late on the scene this morning, and thereby witnessed a most extraordinary scene. Some six or seven killer whales, old and young, were skirting the fast floe ahead of the ship. . . ."

Scott had hoped the weather and other items of chance would be in his favor; but now that the base was established, and his depots placed in order, everything seemed to go wrong. Although advised to rely on dogs, Scott felt that ponies could pull the sleds over longer distances without tiring. In order that his ponies might be prepared for the cold, he had had them hardened on the steppes of Siberia.

This decision was a major mistake. The ponies were terrified by the snow and ice. They stampeded and broke their legs in the many crevasses and had to be shot. What dogs they had—big huskies from the Yukon—failed to perform as expected. Some went wild. Others fell into the deep cracks that crossed the glaciers.

And then word came that his friendly rival, Amundsen, had established a base at the Bay of Whales. This meant that the Norwegian was headed for the South Pole. But Scott merely winced for a moment. With courage, he wrote: "One thing fixes itself definitely in my mind . . . to go forward and do our best for honor of the country without fear or panic."

The race was on!

Without animals to help them, Scott and four of his men harnessed themselves to a thousand-pound sled and headed for the South Pole—the final objective of all their dreams. The going was rough. Blizzards from the vast white silence whistled down on them, lashing and cutting their faces.

Pulling the sled in the thin atmosphere, more than 10,000 feet above sea level, drained what small energy they had left after a year and a half of struggle, pain, and homesickness. But the hope of being the first to set foot on the Pole drove them on like a scourge. Knowing the value of diaries, Scott forced himself to note their progress.

"Thursday, January 11. Height 10,530. T 25.8 degrees.

About 74 miles from the Pole—can we keep this up for seven days? It takes it out of us like anything. None of us ever had such hard work before."

Five days later, shattering disappointment faced the group. But though gripped by near-despair, Scott jotted down the facts.

"Tuesday, January 16. Camp 68. Height 9,760. T 23.5 degrees. The worst has happened or nearly the worst . . . Bowers' sharp eyes detected what he thought was a cairn (a heap of stones). . . . Soon we knew it could be no natural snow feature. We marched on, found that it was a black flag tied to a sledge bearer. . . . All the daydreams must go. . . ."

Still there was hope, a chance in a million that by some curious fate they could manage to be first to that most difficult spot. Scott filled his lungs with the rare, frigid air, gripped the Union Jack and prayed. He forced his bone-weary feet to go on and strained his eyes. Then he and his companions saw what they had hoped they would never see. Choking back emotions, Scott noted it down.

"Thursday morning, January 18. Decided after summing up all observations that we are 3.5 miles from the Pole . . . . Bowers saw a . . . tent. . . . In the tent we find a record of five Norwegians having been here. . . ."

Amundsen had beaten them to the Pole! There could be no doubt about it. Scott left a note in the tent. Then he went ahead to what he considered to be the very center of the Pole and fastened the Union Jack to a piece of stick.

With the use of dog teams, the Norwegians had reached the South Pole on December 16, 1911. Scott, arriving on January 17, 1912, had been beaten by approximately one month. His last sentence in his diary on that searing day of disappointment is a masterpiece of courageous acceptance. "Well, we have turned our back now on that goal of our ambition and must face the 800 miles of solid dragging—and good-bye to most of our daydreams."

The way back was filled with heartbreaking disaster. Evans—perhaps the strongest—slipped on the ice, crushed his skull and died. Oates' feet were so frostbitten he could barely keep up. Knowing that he was hindering the others, he calmly announced: "I am going outside. I may be gone for some time." He never returned and his body was never found.

Staggering, stumbling, hoping, praying, Scott and his two survivors kept going. Their faces and feet froze and became brittle. The miles before them stretched out, and out, and out. The white silences of snow and ice and wind and crevices mocked them. But they continued on, hoping for an impossible break. If only the weather would change!

Scott's last entry was on Thursday, March 29. "Since the 21st we have had a continuous gale . . . . We had fuel to make two cups of tea apiece and bare food for two days on the 20th. Every day we have been ready to start for our depot 11 miles away, but outside the door of the tent it remains a scene of whirling drift . . . . We shall stick it out to the end, but we are getting weaker, of course, and the end cannot be far.

"It seems a pity, but I do not think I can write more."

Then, remembering his wife and little Peter, he added a postscript. "For God's sake look after our people."

Eight months later, those who found the bodies also found the diaries. They buried the men under two skis lashed together in the form of a cross. Over the grave, they wrote some words of Tennyson which included this magnificent line:

To strive, to seek, to find, but not to yield.

Twenty-two years later England, thinking of Scott, built the first polar museum in the world. Across the front of the building they inscribed a dedication to their dead hero. The translation from the Latin reads: "He sought the secrets of the Pole, He found the secrets of God."

7

"Here I Stand"

As Martin Luther rested at the Hospital of the Knights of St. John on the sunny morning of April 18, 1521, the events of the previous day hammered at his mind. He had been pleased with what he had said to the emperor and his court at the Diet of Worms, but the worst was far from over.

He could still see the dust and hear the noise of the thousands of Germans, Italians, and Spaniards who elbowed each other to get a glimpse of him. The soldiers had had great difficulty in pushing the milling crowd back enough so he could enter the appointed hall.

Standing near the tall, heavy doors of that building had been the famous German general, George of Freundsberg, who had captured the king of France four years ago. The old warrior had touched Luther on the shoulder and said: "Poor monk! Poor monk! Thou art now going to make a far nobler stand than I or any other captains have made in the bloodiest of battles! But if thy cause is just, and thou art sure of it, go forward in God's name, and fear nothing. God will not forsake thee!"

Then, as the guards led him toward the front, a friendly prince whispered: "Fear not them which kill the body, but are not able to kill the soul." Another man of equally high rank, added: "When ye shall be brought before governors and kings for my sake, the spirit of your Father shall speak in you."

Moments later, with the eyes of the vast assembly locked onto his stout features, Martin Luther stood in front of the newly-elected Emperor of the Holy Roman Empire, Charles V. Although this pale young man on the throne was merely 20 years old, he ruled a sprawling empire second only to the empire of Charlemagne. Surrounding him were his brother, Archduke Ferdinand, twenty-four dukes, six electors of the empire, ambassadors and secular leaders, as well as thirty archbishops, bishops and abbots.

The 204 who formed the court represented more power than could be assembled elsewhere on the earth.

"Say nothing until you are questioned," ordered the marshal of the empire sternly as he scowled at Luther.

Following a painful silence, Marshal John Eck began to speak in a voice both fierce and solemn. "Martin Luther! His sacred and invincible imperial majesty has cited you before his throne, in accordance with the advice and counsel of the states of the Holy Roman Empire, to require of you to answer two questions: First, do you acknowledge these books to have been written by you?"

Eck then pointed to a table in the middle of the hall on which twenty of Luther's publications were piled. "Second, are you prepared to retract those books, and their contents, or do you persist in the opinions you have advanced in them?"

Luther started to reply when he was interrupted by his counsel, Jerome Schurff. "Let the titles of the books be read!" said the attorney.

Methodically, Eck began to read the titles—many of which were devotional books. And then, his voice raised slightly, he read the name of Luther's most controversial tract, "The Babylonian Captivity."

It was an overt attack on the pope and five of the seven sacraments proclaimed by the Roman Catholic Church. Indeed, it was so pointed and filled with invective, it had prompted Erasmus to cry out: "The breach is irreparable."

The last title having been read, Luther replied: "Most gracious emperor! Gracious princes and lords! His imperial majesty has asked me two questions. As to the first, I acknowledge as mine the books that have just been named: I cannot deny them.

"As to the second, seeing that it is a question that concerns faith and the salvation of souls, and in which the Word of God, the greatest and most precious treasure either in heaven or earth, is interested, I should act imprudently were I to reply without reflection. I might affirm less than the circumstance demands, or more than the truth requires, and so sin against this saying of Christ: 'Whosoever shall deny me before men, him will I also deny before my Father which is in heaven.' For this reason I entreat your imperial majesty, with all humility, to allow me time, that I may answer without offending the Word of God."

After a brief court discussion, Luther was given another day to prepare an answer. The only stipulation was that he answer vocally rather than by letter.

The imperial herald would summon him sometime in the afternoon to again face the emperor. Martin Luther was deeply concerned that he do and say just the right things to please God.

His experiences on his journey from Wittenberg would

have stopped a less courageous man. At Naumburg a sympathetic priest brought out a portrait of Savonarola and held it up to him. Savonarola had been burned at the stake in Florence by the order of Pope Alexander VI. A comment was unnecessary.

In another city, while people flocked around him, one of them said: "Ah! there are so many bishops and cardinals at Worms! . . . They will burn you and reduce your body to ashes, as they did John Hus."

Luther replied: "Though they should kindle a fire all the way from Worms to Wittenberg, the flames of which reached to heaven, I would walk through it in the name of the Lord—I would appear before them—I would enter the jaws of this behemoth, and break his teeth, confessing the Lord Jesus."

Luther knew, however, that words are cheap, and that flames and prison are real. Within minutes he would be facing an inexperienced young man whose nod could send him to the stake. And although the emperor had signed a document guaranteeing safe conduct, the guarantee was good for only 21 days. Moreover, he remembered that a century before, John Hus had received a similar document —but the Emperor Sigismund flagrantly violated his word, and ordered Hus to be burned and his bones to be ground into bits and tossed into the Rhine.

As was his habit in moments of crisis, Luther went to the Lord in prayer. The hour of testing drew near; he placed his left hand on the Word, and lifting his right hand, promised that he would be faithful.

Because of the crowds, a larger hall was selected. Luther was not allowed to appear until early evening. The building was lit with torches. Martin Luther stood before the emperor's throne and waited.

Soon John Eck addressed him, repeating the questions

of the previous day. This time Luther was ready. "Most serene emperor, most illustrious princes, most clement lords, if I have not given some of you your proper titles I beg you to forgive me. I am not a courtier, but a monk. You asked me yesterday whether the books were mine and whether I would repudiate them. They are all mine, but as for the second question, they are not all of one sort."

Luther's voice was calm, resonant, clear. As he spoke, he was confident the Lord was helping him. "I confess I have been more caustic than comports with my profession, but I am being judged, not on my life, but for the teaching of Christ, and I cannot renounce these works wither, without increasing tyranny and impiety."

Eck listened impatiently as Luther went on with his lengthy speech. Then he turned fiercely on him: "I ask you, Martin—answer candidly without horns—do you or do you not repudiate your books and the errors which they contain?"

The only sound came from the sputtering of the torches as Luther swept his eyes over the magnificent court.

"Since then your Majesty and your lordships desire a simple reply, I will answer without horns and without teeth. Unless I am convinced by Scripture and plain reason—I do not accept the authority of popes and councils, for they have contradicted each other—my conscience is captive to the Word of God. I cannot and I will not recant anything, for to go against conscience is neither right nor safe."

All eyes were riveted on him; everyone was leaning forward, some with their hands to their ears. No one wanted to miss a word.

Then with a silent prayer churning in his heart, Luther cried: "Here I stand, I can do no other; may God help me! Amen!"

Several weeks later, the Diet of Worms pronounced

Martin Luther a heretic. But by this time he was hidden away at Wartburg Castle and was beginning his translation of the Greek New Testament into German—a translation that survives until this day.

8

Robert Moffat and the Outlaw

Robert Moffat headed straight for Government House even though he knew Governor Lord Charles Somerset despised missionaries—especially young ones.

Although completely lacking in higher education, Moffat felt that as a son of God, he should fear no one. With this confidence, his highly polished boots clicked over the cobblestone streets of Capetown to keep the appointment with his Lordship.

The Governor knew he had to tolerate some missionaries in the colony because of circumstances. But he was determined not to encourage anyone to come to South Africa in order to start new works, particularly in new areas. In a curt letter to the Colonial Secretary, he said: "I am disposed to think no further encouragement at present be given to missionary establishments beyond the boundary. . . ."

During the 85-day voyage from England, Moffat's heart

had been churning to preach the Gospel to new tribes. His board, The London Missionary Society, had been working mostly with Hottentots for more than 20 years. But Moffat wondered about the people up north.

As Moffat and the five other missionaries gingerly entered the office, he prayed the Governor would give them permission to head north.

His Lordship, however, was obstinate. He seemed determined to believe that the mission stations were providing hiding places for runaway slaves. One of the missionaries pleaded that it was not their intention "to teach the people to be rebellious but to submit to the powers that be." The unconvinced Governor, however, lost all interest. Slavery was a very real problem in South Africa when this interview took place on January 17, 1817.

While waiting for an open door, Moffat began to hear amazing stories about Jager Afrikaner, the notorious outlaw.

Afrikaner, along with other black Africans, had lost his land in the northern push of the Boers as they tried to escape domination by the British at Capetown.

But while others fled, Afrikaner and his clan remained. They worked for a Dutch farmer. Small frictions mounted into a scuffle, during which Jager's brother killed the farmer. Knowing the consequences, the entire group fled across the Orange and set up a kingdom of their own in Namaqualand. Jager became the chief, and his main occupation became that of sweeping down on the people of the south. Robbery and murder became his passion; his name came to be feared in South Africa much as the name of Jesse James was feared in America years later.

While Moffat was studying Dutch and doing evangelistic work, a rumor drifted down that Jager had been converted, joined the mission, and had even changed his name to Christian Afrikaner. Few believed it, but Robert Moffat was intrigued. From his own experience he knew the human heart could be changed. And he determined that one way or another he would cross the Orange and shake Jager's hand. When one of the plump Dutch wives heard this, she scoffed: "He will make a drinking cup out of your skull."

Robert Moffat was unimpressed by such stories.

Moffat was born in the home of a Scottish ploughman on December 21, 1795. Since higher education seemed unattainable, he was apprenticed to a gardener at 14. It seemed this would be his life's work. But all was changed when he moved to England at 18. While working as a gardener and keeping a series of 19 fires going in the greenhouses, he attended a tiny meeting conducted by Independent Methodists at High Legh. He earnestly sought Christ, but seek as he would, he could not feel the definite assurance of salvation.

Then, while studying the letter to the Romans on his own, he suddenly saw the way. Joyfully he remembered: "I felt that being justified by faith, I had peace with God through the Lord Jesus Christ."

While still in the glow of this experience, he noticed a placard advertising that William Roby of Manchester was to speak at a missionary meeting at Warrington. He attended and was deeply stirred to become a missionary.

Learning that Roby had a school for prospective ministers and missionaries, Moffat got a job as a gardener from James Smith at Dukinfield. This enabled him to attend Roby's church in nearby Manchester and take his course in divinity. The move to Dukinfield had another blessing, for while he was there he fell in love with his employer's daughter, Mary Smith. And as it often happens in the Lord's will, William Roby was a director of the London Missionary Society.

Roby believed in Moffat, and soon arranged for his appointment to South Africa. Everything was perfect except that Mary could not get her father's permission to marry the young would-be missionary, and sail with him to Africa.

At the end of seven months, the Governor finally agreed that Moffat, along with Mr. and Mrs. Kitchingman, could go to Namaqualand. After all, the country was mostly desert, and what harm could they do? Even runaway slaves would have more intelligence than to flee up there.

In October, Moffat and the Kitchingmans loaded their wagons and headed for Afrikaner country. The wagons were pulled by oxen, and since it was likely that some oxen would perish on the way, a number of spares tagged along behind. As the wagon started out, a lady bade them farewell. "Had you been an old man," she said to Moffat, blotting her tears with the corner of her apron, "it would have been nothing, for you would have died sooner or no; but you are young and are going to become a prey to that monster!"

With no hotels or inns available, the travelers followed the South African custom of stopping at a Dutch farm house on the way. Often in these homes Moffat was asked to lead the worship service, for most of the Dutch were highly religious even though they did very little to take the Gospel to the natives.

Having crossed the 500-yard-wide Orange, Moffat came face to face with the famous outlaw. After he had grasped his hand, he was convinced by his manner that he indeed had been converted. Soon Moffat and Afrikaner were close friends. Moffat helped the former outlaw read his Dutch Bible and explained difficult passages. The two worked together, planned together, and operated a school together. Sometimes Moffat sat up late, and while playing his violin would listen to Afrikaner's stories. Years later, he remembered an unusual occasion:

"One day when seated together I happened in absence of mind to be gazing steadfastly at him. It arrested his attention, and he modestly enquired the cause. I replied: 'I was trying to picture to myself your carrying fire and sword through the country, and I could not think how eyes of yours could smile at human woe.' Afrikaner shed a flood of tears."

While working with the former outlaw, Moffat received a letter from Mary Smith, telling him that her father absolutely refused to let her leave England. It seemed his whole world had been blown apart. Then, after writing a long letter to his parents, he suddenly conceived a brilliant idea.

He decided to take Christian Afrikaner to Capetown and prove to Lord Somerset that missionary work paid, and that all missionaries were not a sickly collection of fuddy-duddies.

"But there's a price on my head!" complained Afrikaner, spreading his hands in horror.

"Oh, but I'll take care of you; and God will help. . . ."

After three days of prayer, Afrikaner agreed on the single stipulation that he could dress as Moffat's servant. This would help him get by many Dutch homes where he had committed atrocities.

At one farm the Dutch owner refused to shake hands with Moffat. "Who are you?" he demanded brusquely.

"I'm Robert Moffat. I—"

"Moffat!" exploded the man with a shaky voice. "It—it is your g-ghost," he concluded, backing away.

"I'm no ghost."

"Don't come near me—"

"But I'm no ghost." Moffat rubbed his hands as proof.

"Everyone says that you were murdered by Afrikaner; and a man told me he had seen your bones!"

In time, the Dutchman held out his hand. But he was still skeptical. "When did you rise from the dead?" he demanded.

"I was never dead. Afrikaner is now a Christian!"

"Well, if what you assert be true respecting that man, I have only one wish, and that is to see him before I die; and when you return as sure as the sun is over our heads, I will go with you to see him, though he killed my own uncle."

Just then Afrikaner stepped up and Moffat introduced him. The Dutchman asked a few questions for assurance, and then with bulging eyes, he nearly shouted: "O God, what a miracle of Thy power! What cannot Thy grace accomplish!"

Back in Capetown, Moffat carefully polished his boots. Then with Afrikaner in tow, he went clicking over the cobbled streets to the Governor's mansion. At first his Lordship stared at the tamed outlaw in utter disbelief. Convinced at last, he expressed his satisfaction by presenting Afrikaner with the huge reward that had been on his head. He also gave him a full pardon and a letter guaranteeing his safety back to the frontier!

This startling accomplishment opened bolted doors for Moffat. Permission was granted at once for him to start a new mission to the north. In addition to this great news, Mary Smith wrote that she had received permission from her father to come to Africa.

Six months later, Robert Moffat and Mary Smith were married. They spent their honeymoon in an ox wagon heading north.

9

The "Peculiar" Preacher

Uncle Bob Sheffey strode briskly up to the cabin on Wolfe Creek where the man had been bitten by a rattlesnake. He had tried to win this family to the Lord for a long time, but his efforts had been scorned. Now in emergency they had called him. This day, he decided, was a rare day—a day of unique opportunity.

Flinging wide the door of the crude cabin, Sheffey noted that a doctor had already been there and that the victim would live. He sank to his knees and prayed: "O Lord, we do thank Thee for rattlesnakes. If it had not been for a rattlesnake they would not have called on You. Send a rattlesnake to bite Bill, and one to bite John, and send a great big one to bite the old man!"

The family was not unduly shocked by that prayer. They knew Uncle Bob, and they knew he was deeply concerned for the salvation of their souls. Moreover, they knew this slender, circuit-riding Methodist preacher would give anything—even his life—if he felt it would help them. He was of their kind and they loved him. And now they listened with respect as he preached and warned them that "today is the day of salvation."

Although Sheffey has been dead for about 75 years, his fame lingers on in the blue hills of southwestern Virginia. The natives speak of him in hushed tones, and if a speaker is losing his crowd, all he has to do is mention the name of this eccentric preacher and the people lean forward.

Uncle Bob was not a fluent speaker. One man recalled: "Brother Sheffey was the most powerful man in prayer I ever heard, but he couldn't preach a lick." Nevertheless, when it was announced that Sheffey was going to preach, the little frame buildings were usually crowded to the doors. Sheffey's prayers were often answered in the most dramatic way—and he always said precisely what he thought. Sometimes his quaint thoughts had barbs in them, but that didn't concern him.

His petitions to the Lord were uncomfortably long, and because of this he was ignored for several days at a ministers' meeting. Finally, one thoughtful clergyman asked him to lead in prayer. With his bearded face lifted toward the heavens, he prayed: "O Lord, Thou knowest that this Thy servant has been here all these days, and those here have not recognized him as Thy servant; and now, Lord, I don't know what Thou thinkest of them, but as for me I think they are small potatoes and few in the hill."

Bob Sheffey had seen the evils of drink in his circuit and was very much against it. One day as he was riding near Wolfe Creek he noticed some men building a new still. Dismounting quickly, he tethered his horse, spread out a sheepskin to protect his knees, and offered a long prayer which he finished by requesting that the Lord "smash the still into smithereens." He then got up, smoothed his trousers—he was always very neat—and

Photo by Charles Ludwig

Dr. Charles Tindley managed to teach himself to read, and worked his way up from slave to preacher in one of the nation's largest Presbyterian churches.

This relief of Hus is part of a memorial stone, placed near the rooms where he was arrested.

This monument to the reformer, John Hus, was erected in downtown Prague.

Photos by Charles Ludwig

Photo by Wilbur Kirby

"The Old Rugged Cross" was written in 1913 by George Bennard.

Mr. and Mrs. Frank Virgil were members of the first choir to sing "The Old Rugged Cross."

Photo by
Charles Ludwig

Plate IV
Photo by Charles Ludwig

British Museum Photo

This family monument to William Hatfield (Devil Anse) was imported from Italy at a cost of $3000. It was pulled to the cemetery by a team of mules.

Robert Falcon Scott, as he needed to dress when he made his historic journey to the South Pole.

British Museum Photo

John Newton, who had picked up the nickname "The Old African Blasphemer," went on to write such hymns as "Amazing Grace" for his congregation in Olney.

Photo by Charles Ludwig

Photo by Charles Ludwig

Dr. Martin Luther, as depicted in a painting at Worms, Germany—the city in which he was condemned as a heretic.

Robert Moffat, left, kept this drawing of Jager Afrikaner, right, in one of his books.

London Missionary Society Photo

This tapestry of a Dutch family is from the same period in South African history as Moffat's tour of missionary duty, during which the outlaw Afrikaner became a Christian.

Photo by Charles Ludwig

Photo by Charles Ludwig

Religious News Service Photo

John Calvin is shown being challenged by William Farel to come to Geneva, Switzerland, with him. Farel wished to make Geneva into a truly Protestant city during the Reformation.

Pearisburg Church Photo

The preacher "Uncle Bob" Sheffey—
from a photograph in his church
near Pearisburg, Va.

British Museum Photo

William Cowper, shown above, collaborated with John Newton on the famous hymnbook, the Olney Hymns.

William Booth, right, founded the Salvation Army in 1865, and is shown preaching to the poverty-stricken masses of London's East End.

Plate XIII
Salvation Army Photo

Hull Museum Photos

William Wilberforce, who triggered England's abolition of the slave trade, built a model of a slaver so Parliament could see the crowded conditions that often killed 20% of the slaves on their way to the West Indies.

The heart of Dr. David Livingstone was buried next to a Mvulu tree, on which the date of his death was carved.

Livingstone—as he appeared during his early days in Africa.

continued on his way with complete confidence that his prayer would be answered.

Within a week, a heavy tree fell on the still and wrecked it. The owner, however, was not a man to give up easily. Within a few days he started to rebuild. When Sheffey heard about this, he knelt on his sheepskin and prayed again. This time a flash flood did the job—and did it so thoroughly not a board was left in place.

At another ministers' meeting when everyone seemed to be at odds, the chairman asked Sheffey to pray. "Lord, I think I know what the trouble is. I am sure the devil is here, and I want You to take him by the nape of the neck, and take him to the edge of the cliff out here, and kick him off," prayed Sheffey.

This prayer was apparently answered, for immediately a wonderful spirit of surrender and cooperation took over the entire assembly, and many ministers received new inspiration.

Appropriately Sheffey was born on July 4, 1820, in Ivanhoe, Virginia. His parents were solid citizens who earned their living from the land. An uncle was elected to Congress and a brother became a well-known judge. He lost his mother when he was only a child, and was entrusted to an aunt who lived in Abingdon, Virginia. He was converted in a Methodist revival there at the age of 19.

Feeling his call to the ministry, he enrolled almost at once in Emory and Henry College. But study bored him. Before the year was out he was riding the hills of Virginia doing missionary work. A minister who met him during those years published this impression.

"We found R. S. Sheffey, who had been trying to get a license to preach for several years and failed, because he was a peculiar man. We succeeded in having him licensed to preach, and then kept him with us for three years. He spends about two thirds of his waking hours in prayer. His prayers are very frequently answered immediately! And in nothing more frequently than for the downfall of establishments for intemperance."

Sheffey was at his best during a Methodist class meeting. He loved to say, "I've been born twice—of the flesh on July 4, 1820; and of the Spirit on January 9, 1839, over Greenway's store, at Abingdon, Virginia."

Whenever it was known that he was visiting a community, all the houses would open to him. After he was gone, the people would discuss his words for weeks. His favorite dish was chicken and dumplings, and he had a way of advertising his taste wherever he went. Once, when asked to say grace, he prayed: "Lord, we thank Thee for this good woman; we thank Thee for this good dinner—but it would be better if the chicken had dumplings in it. Amen."

He hated to leave a home without reading the Bible and having prayer with the family. On one of these occasions, a neighbor girl joined the little worship circle he was leading. And so in his prayer, he said: "God bless this little girl with the red 'joisey' on, and God bless Tommy. We want them to get married."

Again the prayer was answered. The girl grew up and married Tommy and they became Reverend and Mrs. Thomas Priddy!

Sheffey refused to be concerned by those who ridiculed him. But even they had a secret admiration for his success. In his autobiography, Dr. George C. Rankin wrote: "He could say the oddest things, hold the most unique interviews with God, break forth in the most unexpected spasms of prayer, use the homeliest illustrations, do the funniest things and go through with the most grotesque performances of any man born to woman.

"It was just 'Bob Sheffey,' and nobody thought of anything he did or said, except to let him have his way and to do exactly what he pleased. In anybody else it would not have been tolerated for a moment. In fact, he acted more like a crazy man than otherwise, but he was wonderful in a meeting. He would stir the people, crowd the mourner's bench with crying penitents and have genuine conversions by the score. I doubt if any man in all that conference has as many souls to his credit in the Lamb's Book of Life as old Bob Sheffey."

In spite of all this unique admiration, his brother, Judge Sheffey, got a little exasperated with him. "Bob," he admonished, "I want you to stop being so peculiar."

"I won't do it," replied Bob, "for the Bible says that God's people are a peculiar people."

"Yes, but there is no use in being childish!"

"Oh, yes, there is, for the Bible says, 'that except ye be converted and become as little children, ye shall not enter the kingdom of God.'"

On a lazy afternoon while riding to an appointment, Sheffey noticed a wide shelf rock—an ideal place for a Gospel sign. Dismounting, he wrote in huge letters: "What must I do to be saved?"

Coming back several weeks later, Sheffey found that a patent medicine man had written beneath his question in equally large letters: "Use Hite's Pain Cure." But the clever salesman did not have the last word, for in even larger letters, Sheffey added: "AND PREPARE TO MEET THY GOD!"

Bob refused to retire. Indeed, the people would not let him. He was still preaching when the Lord summoned him at the age of 82.

His grave is in the Wesley Chapel graveyard near Pearisburg, Virginia. The inscription at the bottom of the stone indicates what people thought of him.

> "Fully consecrated to God's service, he preached the Gospel, without money and without price, and has entered upon his reward. The poor were sorry he died."

10

The Absent-Minded Poet

Today, his home at Olney, just north of London, is a museum; every year thousands stream through the red brick house to see where he lived and worked. They can view the iron grates used in his fireplaces, the rush-bottom chairs on which he sat, the desk at which he composed his immortal poetry, and a shelf of books written about him.

Perhaps the most interesting item in the quaint building is a painting which shows the absent-minded poet boiling his watch for breakfast while thoughtfully holding the egg. Historians remember that William Cowper (pronounced Cooper) had repeated attacks of insanity. Indeed, he spent 18 months in an insane asylum. Nevertheless, he wrote such imperishable hymns as "There Is a Fountain Filled with Blood," "O For a Closer Walk with God," and "God Moves in a Mysterious Way."

Cowper was one of the world's truly great poets. His lines stand shoulder to shoulder with those of Wordsworth, Tennyson, and Robert Burns. Yet his life was one of the most tormented lives of any of the great men of letters. On several occasions he attempted suicide, and had it not been for his conversion, he would probably have tried until he succeeded.

William Cowper was born in a preacher's home at Great Berkhamstead in Herefordshire on November 26, 1731. His father, the Reverend John Cowper, D.D., was a man of considerable importance.

But the Cowper home was not always a happy one. Of the seven children, only two survived infancy. Cowper's mother died after the last child was born. Although William was only six when his mother died, he had strong memories of her, and thought of her with sentimental nostalgia the rest of his life. His mother was a distant relative of John Donne, and she had inherited the poet's sensitivity which she passed on to William.

Berkhamstead was a little agricultural town of 1,500. There were beautiful tree-lined lanes, the ruins of a castle and a bubbling creek. Young William was completely in love with the place; but his father, following the fashion of the day, decided that he should be sent away to school.

At Bedfordshire, a 15-year-old lad, noticing William's extreme shyness, specialized in picking on him. He bullied him until William was completely cowed—his nerves shattered. In later years Cowper had no memory of the boy's face; all he could remember were the buckles of his dreadful shoes. Later, the bully was expelled, but the damage had already been done.

In a short memoir William remembered: "One day as I was sitting alone on a bench in the school, melancholy, and almost ready to weep at the recollection of what I had already suffered, and expecting the same from my tormentor every moment, these words of the Psalmist came into my mind, 'I will not be afraid of what man can do to me.' I applied this to my own case . . . . Instantly, I perceived in myself a new briskness of spirits, and a cheerfulness which I had never before experienced . . . . Happy had it been for me, if this early effort toward dependence on God had been repeated by me. But, alas! it was the first and last instance of this kind between infancy and manhood."

Cowper soon developed a weakness in his eyes. The trouble may have been aggravations brought on by the bully. He left school and went to live with an irreligious doctor and his wife for two years. But the doctor was unable to help him.

He then enrolled at Westminster. Dr. Cowper dreamed that his son would make a good lawyer. Although William abhorred the idea, he signed up as an apprentice to Mr. Chapman—an attorney at Holburn. William despised the work, but he stayed on in order to please his father. In 1754 he was admitted to the bar as a member of the Inner Temple.

At the death of his father, William received an inheritance, but it was so small he had to go to work at once. Friends arranged for him to be employed in a minor position in the House of Lords. But in order to secure the position, it was necessary for him to take an examination.

This examination was a mere formality—but as Cowper worried about it, it grew in his mind until he was overwhelmed. Finally, he lost his mind. He became so upset he bought some poison, but he lacked the courage to take it. Then he unsheathed a knife. Again, however, he failed to press it home.

His concerned friends now had him confined to an insane asylum at St. Albans. He was fortunate that Dr. Cotton, the owner and manager, was an enthusiastic Christian. Also, he wrote poetry, and was an excellent story teller. He and Cowper became warm friends, and the therapy of exchanging stories did the troubled man a lot of good.

Unfortunately, Cowper suffered under the delusion that

there was no salvation for him. He spoke in solemn tones of his "irrevocable doom," and refused to believe that salvation was for "whosoever." While in this morbid frame of mind, he was visited by his brother John. William never forgot that visit; it was like a beacon to a lost sailor.

"As soon as we were left alone, he asked me how I found myself; I answered, 'As much better as despair can make me.' We went together into the garden. Here on expressing a settled assurance of judgment, he protested to me that it was all a delusion; and protested so strongly, that I could not help giving some attention to him. I burst into tears and cried out, 'If it be a delusion, then am I the happiest of beings.' Something like a ray of hope was shot into my heart; but still I was afraid to indulge it. We dined together, and I spent the afternoon in a more cheerful manner. Something seemed to whisper to me, 'Still there is mercy.'"

A few days later he received another jog in the right direction. "Having found a Bible on the bench in the garden, I opened upon the 11th chapter of John where Lazarus is raised from the dead; and saw so much benevolence, mercy, goodness, and sympathy with miserable men, in our Saviour's conduct, that I almost shed tears on the relation . . . . I sighed, and said, 'Oh, that I had not rejected a good Redeemer, that I had not forfeited all his favors.' Thus was my heart softened, though not yet enlightened."

But still hoping and praying, he opened the Bible again, and this time he read: "Whom God hath set forth to be a propitiation through faith in his blood, to declare his righteousness for the remission of sins that are past, through the forbearance of God" (Romans 3: 25).

This passage unlocked the door. Immediately he received the assurance of his salvation. He became so enthusiastic about his sudden release, he dashed off a 13 verse poem, the first verse of which is this:

> All at once my chains were broken,
>   From my feet the fetters fell,
> And the word in pity spoken
>   Snatched me from the jaws of hell.
>   Sweet the sound of grace divine,
>   Sweet the grace that makes it mine.

Cowper was now recovering swiftly. But Dr. Cotton had been so kind to him, he hated to leave. The quiet routine in the E-shaped building with its restful gardens appealed to him. Had it not been for the expense, which his friends were meeting, he might have remained there the rest of his life!

After a number of years of shifting about, Cowper took rooms with Mrs. Unwin, the widow of a minister at Olney. He was especially attracted to this place, for John Newton was the pastor. Each Sunday found Cowper sitting in the gallery absorbing the Gospel as proclaimed by the former slaver. But even though he had enjoyed a stable period of tranquility, the old doubts began to haunt him.

Alarmed that Cowper might have to return to St. Albans, Newton asked him to collaborate with him on a new hymnal—a hymnal that would proclaim the good news in an easily understood manner. Soon Cowper was busy, and as he wrote, signing each completed hymn with a "C," his old buoyancy returned.

Neither Newton nor Cowper realized it, but their forthcoming *Olney Hymns* was to become a world-renowned classic.

Cowper never preached, but he did share in visitation and in the distribution of charity. He and Newton used to walk together as they worked the streets.

Cowper was inclined to be indolent, so his writing often came from sudden inspiration. One of these resulted from a serious illness suffered by his landlady. Cowper remembered: "She is the chief blessing I have met with in my journey since the Lord was pleased to call me . . . I began to compose the verses yesterday morning before daybreak but fell asleep after the first two lines; when I awakened again, the third and fourth were whispered to my heart in a way which I have often experienced." The hymn was the familiar "O For a Closer Walk with God," written in 1779.

Altogether, the Olney Hymnal contained 68 hymns written by Cowper. One of the best known is "There Is a Fountain Filled with Blood." Today, some are repelled by the stark realism of the hymn, but having had a dramatic conversion, the lines were exceedingly real to Cowper. The fourth verse was his personal testimony.

> E're since by faith I saw the stream
> Thy flowing wounds supply,
> Redeeming love has been my theme,
> And shall be till I die.

Following the publication of the hymnal, brighter days came to Cowper. His long poem, "The Task," which extolled the virtues of rural living, met with success and provided royalties. But he was never able to earn an adequate living. Had it not been for a pension arranged by friends, he would have been a pauper.

His mind continued to trouble him the rest of his life. There would be long stretches of sunny confidence and then days of formidable gloom. His troubles increased in the spring of 1800 when he was seized by dropsy. Dr. John Johnson came to spend time with him. As the pastor spoke of a "merciful Redeemer," Cowper stopped him.

His mind was in turmoil again!

Soon he became unconscious. Hours later, he passed away so quietly the minister did not notice. But when he saw that the breathing had stopped, he looked at the face; it was one "of calmness and composure, mingled as it were with holy surprise."

When friends peered into his once troubled face, they were reminded of the fifth verse of one of his hymns:

> Then in a nobler sweeter song,
>   I'll sing thy power to save,
> When this poor lisping, stammering tongue
>   Lies silent in the grave.

11

The Inflexible Man

Few are neutral about John Calvin. Either his doctrine is loved or hated, with great passion on both sides.

Nevertheless, this sickly, cadaverous-looking man did as much as anyone to shape the Reformation. Just as the uneducated quote Shakespeare without knowing it, all of us—religious or not, Calvinist or not—live different lives than we would have lived had it not been for this iron-willed man of Geneva. Indeed, the very marrow of middle class society stems directly or indirectly from John Calvin.

When Calvin's slender, inflexible fingers wrote, the people read—and paid attention.

On July 10, 1509, Jeanne Caulvin (probably the original French spelling) gave birth to her fourth son, John, at Noyon, the cathedral town of Picardy in northern France. The father, Gerard Calvin, was a moderately well-to-do lawyer who worked as a secretary to the bishop and as an attorney for the cathedral.

Ambitious for his children, Gerard Calvin was determined that all of them, and especially John—the brightest one—should get a thorough education.

Being a devout Catholic and a friend of the bishop, Gerard Calvin secured an income for John. This income was given to him for being the chaplain of one of the altars at the cathedral. At the time, John was not quite 12, and no one expected him to perform any duties. The actual work was done by an old vicar who received only a fraction of John's compensation. In those days such an arrangement was quite usual, and was considered to be something like a scholarship.

At 14, John was sent to the University of Paris to study for the priesthood. It was a difficult school. The food was bad, the rooms were cold, and the teachers frequently beat the students. Classes started at 5 a.m. and continued until 8 p.m. with only four hours of break time.

John, however, took his work so seriously he frequently studied until midnight, and occasionally until dawn. His usual system was to enlarge on his notes, and then memorize them. He loved Latin and the classics, so he came under the care of Mathurin Cordier—a distinguished scholar who was to help him in later life.

John was so sensitive to evil he frequently became quite censorious. The students retaliated by dubbing him "the accusative case." On the whole, however, he was liked.

He finished his course at the University when he was 19. In the meantime, his father had decided that instead of becoming a priest, his brilliant son should become a lawyer, for "the law opened a surer road to riches and honor."

John was now sent to Orleans to study law, later continuing at the University of Bourges. Here, he studied under the famous Italian jurist, Alciati. When he was 22, his father died. This meant that he could drop out of school or change to another profession. But Calvin decided to go ahead with the law, and in due time he was admitted to the bar. But he never practiced law. Instead, he returned to Paris to study the humanities.

While John Calvin was attending the universities, Europe was flaming with Reformation ideas. On October 31, 1517, Luther nailed his 95 theses to the door of All Saints' Church in Wittenberg; and in 1523 Ulrich Zwingli presented his 67 theses.

These were the years that the Inquisition was going at full speed. Those convicted of heresy were burned at the stake—often over a slow fire. Many were put to death on the rack where their joints were pulled apart. Some were beheaded, and many who had been merely accused were locked in dungeons where they awaited their trials for as much as 20 years.

An actual count in 1540 showed that up to that time 20,226 had been burned alive—and this was before Protestantism had become a serious factor.

In spite of this terror, new thought and practice continued to emerge. On October 27, 1523, the town Council of Zurich ordered the abolition of all images and mass celebrations in their churches. This directive was not immediately followed, but the last mass in the city was celebrated on April 12, 1525. The next day, Maundy Thursday, the mass was substituted by a simple communion service.

John Calvin read about these things—and prayed. It took courage to have revolutionary thoughts in those days.

Calvin, however, was listening for God's voice, and in the fall of 1533 he was conscious of a divine directive. He referred to this experience in the preface to his *Commentary on the Psalms*: "God finally curbed and turned me in another direction. Although at first I was so obstinately given to the superstitions of the papacy that it was extremely difficult to drag me from the depths of the mire, yet by sudden conversion He tamed my heart and made it teachable, this heart which for its age was excessively hardened in such matters."

In Paris, Calvin was relatively safe from the Inquisition. King Francis I actually encouraged Humanist attacks on the excesses of the Catholic Church. When his sister Margaret, who had become a Lutheran (the loose word for Protestant), was being attacked by the faculty of the Sorbonne for having written a poem defending Luther, the king sent a note to the University of Paris asking the reason.

Nicholas Cop, recently elected rector of the University, felt that this was an opportunity to witness for Christ. He went to the theological department of the Sorbonne and insisted that the professors stop criticizing Margaret's work. Having success in this, and secretly being a Lutheran himself, he rejoiced. Then he was asked to give his inaugural address on November 1.

How that address was written is a mystery. Some strongly suspect that it was ghostwritten by John Calvin, for a part of it has been preserved in his handwriting. The speech followed the Lutheran line of justification by faith and pleaded for tolerance.

The immediate result was that the University and all of Paris exploded with argument and accusation. Parliament took a stand against the Lutherans and the changeable king joined them. Cop was denounced and had to flee; then accusing fingers pointed at Calvin.

In his hurry to get away, Calvin left all his books and papers in his rooms. Tradition has it that he escaped through a window by means of a rope, then left town disguised as a vinedresser.

Things in Paris soon cooled, and Calvin was able to return quietly. It is thought that he became a consultant on a number of doctrinal matters, and that he even conducted a Protestant communion service.

John Calvin refused the continued income from the

church which his father had first arranged for him. He was arrested twice in Noyon on charges of heresy. Although he spent time in jail twice, the authorities failed to find enough evidence to convict him.

Calvin now fled to Basel. This city had been Protestant for six years, boasted a liberal university, and had a publishing house that was willing to print something new. It was an ideal situation for him.

Many of the leaders of the Reformation had strong doctrinal views; but few of them were good writers. Calvin decided that he would fill this urgent need by writing a systematic book indicating to the world what the Protestants stood for, and at the same time providing a handbook for the emerging Protestant Church.

With these thoughts in mind, he wrote his *Institutes* in 1536.

As the pages piled high on his desk, he wrote with a prayer in his heart and the works of the other reformers stacked around his desk. Soon the first edition of the 520-page *Institutes of the Christian Religion* was on the market, and it caused a sensation. But his own name was not on the book, for he did not want anyone to know that he was the author.

Soon, however, pirated editions were brought out, and these had his name on them. He was now famous, though fame mattered nothing to him. His only concern was truth—as he saw it.

Following the publication of the *Institutes,* Calvin journeyed to Italy and then to Noyon in order to clear up some matters in regard to his father's estate. He had intended to go to Lorraine, but since the direct road to this city was blocked because of war, he went through Geneva instead.

There he was met by William Farel, an undiplomatic zealot who longed to transform Geneva into a Protestant city. He was determined to have the young author stay in Geneva and help him. This Calvin did not want to do, for he longed for a quiet life of writing and study.

Farel, however, was as stubborn as Calvin. Toward morning, he said firmly, "I denounce unto you, in the name of Almighty God, that if, under the pretext of prosecuting your studies, you refuse to labor with us in this work of the Lord, the Lord will curse you, as seeking yourself rather than Christ."

This argument was too much for Calvin; he agreed to move to Geneva. Geneva had a population of around 13,000. It had just thrown off the yoke of the House of Savoy. Nominally it was a Protestant city, thanks to Farel. When Calvin arrived, the city "had neither formal creed nor system of religious training. It had no rights of either property, discipline, revision or membership, or choice or dismisson of pastors."

Calvin's only position in the city was that of pastor. He was also vice-chairman of a consistory "which served as an advisory and liaison body between the Church and civil government." His intellect and personality were so strong, the civil government bent to his will.

With this power, he determined to make Geneva a theocracy. He wrote a set of articles on church government, prepared a catechism for Christian instruction, and penned a Confession of Faith.

Next, he got laws passed that would force the people to live modest Christian lives.

Indecent songs were forbidden. A gambler was publicly pilloried with his cards hanging around his neck. All shops had to be closed on Sunday during worship periods, and everyone was required to attend worship services. This last edict was proclaimed on the streets by trumpet.

Geneva soon tired of Calvin's inflexibility and Farel's lack of tact. In less than two years they were expelled from the city.

But Geneva missed Calvin and summoned him back. He returned three years and four months later.

Calvin remained in Geneva the rest of his life. It was here that he accomplished his greatest work. He revised his *Institutes* five times, and the book grew from six chapters to eighty chapters. His central theme was God's sovereignty—God's greatness and power to control all things. Calvin relentlessly carried his reasoning to conclusions which still form a line of demarcation between doctrinal camps.

But Calvin's doctrines produced mighty men, for they reasoned: "If God has chosen us, we cannot be defeated." A century after Calvin, an essayist wrote, "I had rather meet coming against me a whole regiment with drawn swords than one Calvinist convinced that he is doing the will of God."

During this period, Calvin ruled both the church and Geneva with an iron hand. Moreover, the people accepted his power with respect.

Calvin continued to work all of his life with amazing energy. It is estimated that he preached 286 times each year, besides giving 180 lectures. His prodigious memory enabled him to preach without notes. But since he constantly faced the same congregation, he had to continually come up with fresh material. He also carried on a vast correspondence, labored in civil matters, and wrote commentaries on nearly every book of the Bible.

He drove himself relentlessly in spite of ill health. He founded a university in Geneva which drew students from all over Europe. The school helped supply pastors for the congregations in many nations who were becoming a part of the Reformation.

Calvin believed in honesty, thrift and hard work. He liked to say, "Remember that *time* is money." He also agreed that it was perfectly all right to charge interest for loans, thus contributing to our capitalistic society.

Calvin was only 55 when he passed away, but he looked as if he were 80. He had made strong demands of others, but he had demanded just as much of himself. As a chosen one, he felt that it was his duty to give every ounce of his strength to the Lord—without flinching.

12

The Shrimp Who Grew

There was an expectant stillness in the House of Commons as William Wilberforce leaped to his feet and hurried across the floor to make his speech.

From experience, everyone knew that this tiny shadow of a man was a great speaker. They noted that his head seemed to be screwed a little too deeply into his twisted shoulders, but all he needed was a cause to ignite him into a flame. And on this 12th of May everyone knew that William Wilberforce had a life-consuming cause!

While the House watched this foe of slavery advance toward the speaker's stand, his deformed body reminded them of an observation by James Boswell. "I saw what seemed a mere shrimp mount the table," said the biographer of Sam Johnson, "but as I listened, he grew, and grew, and grew until the shrimp had become a whale." The opposition hoped he would make a fool of himself.

Having been ill when he should have been preparing his

speech, Wilberforce did not have a manuscript. But he ha
lingered on his knees and he felt confident that the Lor
would help him. Then, after surveying the audienc
through half-blind eyes, he made an awkward bow, an
began. As he spoke, his friends prayed that he would d
well. They believed the freedom of the slaves throughou
the British Empire depended on this nearly-dead man.

In the late seventeen and early eighteen hundreds ther
were about 750,000 slaves in the British Empire. Britis
slavers, suffocating with slaves, plowed the seas on thei
way to other countries. Slavery was a festering sore, but
was so profitable Britain's House of Lords determined t
keep it. As always, there was a minority that was ashame
and that wanted to stop the traffic, but this minority wa
unorganized and was up against nearly impossible oppos
tion.

It was even difficult to convince the average man of th
evils of slavery. This was largely because of the Middl
Passage—a system that hid the more sordid details. As th
ships lined up at English ports, preparing to leave fo
Africa, they were loaded with cheap bales of goods
Manchester cloth, second-rate guns, liquor, and beads. I
Africa these items were traded for slaves. When the
returned from the Americas, they returned with We:
Indian sugar and the profits of the slaves. And since th
"black cargo" was never seen by English dock workers o
stockholders, many Englishmen were only vaguely awa
of what was going on.

It was a sinister system. But as always, God chose a ma
to lead the opposition. And although Wilberforce was
semi-invalid most of his life, he was alive with spiritu:
power.

William Wilberforce was born to a wealthy family c
August 24, 1759. The home in which he was reared was

lovely brick mansion, and his mother never tired of relating that Charles I had been entertained there. His father died when William was merely nine; since he was the only child he inherited the fortune. His mother then sent him to Wimbledon, to live with his uncle and aunt.

They were very religious, and greatly admired George Whitefield. These enthusiasms were relayed to William, much to the distress of Mrs. Wilberforce. She did not want her son to be too religious.

Young William hated to return to his mother. But there was no alternative. With him back in Hull, she proceeded to drag him into the society which his uncle and aunt despised. "The theater, balls, great suppers and card parties were the delight of the principal families in town. This mode of life was at first distressing to me, but by degrees I acquired a relish for it." Soon he was far from the Lord.

Following a period at Cambridge where he "wasted as much time as possible," he returned to Hull. "Why don't you run for Parliament?" suggested a friend.

"Run for Parliament? I'm only 21!"

"That makes no difference. George III ascended the throne at 22. And look at his prime minister, William Pitt. He was elected when he was only 24, and nearly everyone agrees that he's the greatest."

The opposition in Hull was formidable. But the Wilberforce name was a good one and he received more votes than his two opponents put together. The House of Commons became a joy—and an excuse for extravagant living. There were dances, gay parties. Sometimes he didn't slump into bed until 4 a.m.

Then in the Christmas season of 1783 he managed to go to church. Lock chapel was a citadel of vital Christianity; and as he listened, memories came swinging back. In his heart he knew the days he had spent with his uncle and aunt were the happiest days of his life.

Two years later, Wilberforce went on a continental trip with Isaac Milner—a thorough Christian. Milner had brought along *The Rise and Progress of Religion in the Soul* by Philip Doddridge. The two discussed the book together. Intrigued, Wilberforce began to study his Greek New Testament, and as he studied the conviction of sin deepened.

Troubled, he went to one of London's more colorful preachers, John Newton—a former slaver. This man, who was later to write "Amazing Grace," led him to Christ. When Wilberforce returned to Parliament, he did so as a reborn Christian. From then on, his entire life was different.

He and Newton continued to have long talks and frequently these talks turned to slavery. "The Old African Blasphemer" related to him the systems used to torture, identify, and transport slaves. He showed him a set of thumbscrews, iron collars, metal-whips, silver branding irons (they caused less infection), and a special apparatus to forcibly feed slaves who were attempting to starve themselves to death. And as Wilberforce listened, his jaws set like a trap. He vowed that he would fight this injustice right up to his last breath. All he wanted was a chance.

From then on Wilberforce lingered on his knees a little longer. One of his prayers was that God would enable him to strike a blow against slavery. And then quite dramatically God answered his prayers. The Prime Minister summoned him to lead the fight in Parliament. Wilberforce recognized his chance and began to prepare for the long struggle ahead. Knowing that he was fighting an entrenched establishment, he summoned experts. The lights in his home continued to burn until late every night as he pored over documents.

As Wilberforce hurled statistics and word pictures at the House of Commons, the members sat as if frozen in their seats. He told them how slaves were so crowded in the holds of the ships that quite often candles could not burn in them because of the lack of oxygen. He described the filth, the disease, the death. The clock ticked on as invective poured from his lips. An hour went by; then two hours; and then three. The House was used to eloquence. But few could speak as an aroused Wilberforce, for as he spoke he saw the slaves, heard the ships, smelled the blood, felt the pain. His lips fairly burned with such sentences as this: "Sir, the nature and all the circumstances of the Trade are now laid open to us. We can no longer plead ignorance. We cannot evade it. We may spurn it. We may kick it out of the way. But we cannot turn aside so as to avoid seeing it." At the end of three and a half hours he dropped into his seat exhausted.

But the opposition was ready. One man said that he would be glad to vote against the Trade if France would lead the way. Another declared that the abolition of slavery would render "the city of London the scene of bankruptcy and ruin."

These were fantastic arguments. But they succeeded in their purpose—that of delaying worthwhile action. Wilberforce was heartsick. His head slumped even deeper into his shoulders and a new siege of illness began. And then he was handed a letter from John Wesley. "Unless God has raised you up for this very thing," wrote the old man, "you will be worn out by the opposition of men and devils. But, if God be with you, who can be against you?' Are all of them stronger than God? O 'be not weary in well doing!' "

Four days later John Wesley was dead, but Wilberforce had received the message. And he didn't forget it even when his resolution was defeated by a vote of 163 to 88.

But the story of his defeat had gotten into the papers, and many allies made themselves known. William Cowper wrote a poem, Josiah Wedgwood made a cameo, John Newton thundered, and King Christian of Denmark was so moved he abolished slavery in his land.

Wilberforce prayed for energy as he organized meeting in the churches. He issued a stream of books and tracts He pleaded with men of influence. Soon public opinion was on his side. Then he had to fight another evil—compromise! Slavery interests, realizing they were losing suggested that "a bounty of five pounds a head" be paid to every slaver whose cargo consisted of more females than males. They also suggested that every female slave be freed after she had raised five children up to the age of seven. The obvious intent of this was to raise slaves so that they would not have to be imported.

Such tactics sickened Wilberforce. They also renewed his determination to keep on with the fight. In and out of the sick bed, he continued to write and to speak. Sometimes it seemed that his crusade was lost—forgotten. But then he would get it going again. He had developed into master of public opinion and refused to quit. Defeat followed defeat. But always he picked himself up. His cause completely dominated his life, his fortune, his career.

Then on May 14, 1833, as Wilberforce was confined to bed because of exhaustion and disease, a new plan was presented. The new bill called for a grant of twenty million pounds to the West Indies to compensate them for their slaves. It also called for complete emancipation within one year. Following emancipation, however, each slave was to serve a twelve-year apprenticeship to his former master. After heated debate the twelve years were reduced to seven years. The bill carried by the slender margin of 15 to 151. But it carried!

The moment Wilberforce was informed, he shouted "Thank God!" By the next day he was strong enough to lead the family in morning prayers, even though he had to be wheeled in. But Sunday night he had another massive attack. He lingered until 3 a.m. Then with a great sigh he passed away. Exactly one year later, on July 31, 1834, some 800,000 slaves were freed.

News of his death brought an immediate request from Parliament that he be buried in Westminster Abbey. At the funeral the old Abbey was jammed to overflowing and the streets for blocks were choked with those who had come to pay their last respects.

His body now lies close to that of William Pitt, the man who shared his hopes, his dreams, his struggles. He deserved the honor, for more than any single person, he helped bring an end to one of the vilest eras in the history of mankind.

13

The Bedridden Dynamo

She twisted painfully in bed, and then with a smile on her pale lips exclaimed, "You need not hurry, Emma! There is plenty of time. I have no train to catch! I have nothing to catch now—only the chariot!"

The pain in her wasted body was terrible, but there was no strain in her voice. She spoke as calmly as if she were dictating an article for the "War Cry."

As the mother of the Salvation Army, Kate Booth had faced dozens of crises, many of them from her sickbed. She had been shackled with illness from girlhood, and her formula for triumph in sorrow was no secret. It had been posted on the wall of her room for all to see: "My grace is sufficient for thee."

Emma patted her mother's cheek and worked a little slower as she dressed the raw flesh around the cancer. Like multitudes of others, she was used to her mother's calmness in times of trial. Newspapers around the world carried the story of Kate's struggle with death. Crowned heads of Europe and starving paupers in great city slums prayed for her. She had become a symbol of hope to the world.

If it had not been for Catherine Booth, or Kate as her husband called her, there might not have been a Salvation Army. She was the inspiration that drove her husband on to victory over almost insurmountable odds. In his later period, when every year brought fresh honors, William gave all of the credit to Kate.

Booth had just started his ministry when he met Catherine Mumford, a member of a congregation where he was the guest preacher. He had noticed her attentiveness and wondered whether it was due to the sermon or the preacher.

That afternoon as he sat across the table from her in the home of his friend Mr. Rabbitts, and peered into her thin face, he knew that it was probably a combination of the two!

Ill health had already wasted Kate's cheeks, even though she was only 23. But as she sat listening to the conversation, her dark eyes snapped with spiritual power. The subject of temperance came up.

This was a delicate subject, for their host was a moderate drinker; nevertheless, Kate strongly took her position. She hated liquor!

Amazed at her spunk, Booth sat back and listened with admiration. Never had he met anyone with so strong a spirit in such a weak body. He decided at once that this girl was for him. Their courtship began immediately. When people suggested that Kate was too frail to be a minister's wife, Booth replied that anyone who could smile at the teeth of trouble as Kate did was strong enough for any man!

Perhaps one reason that Kate was so strong spiritually in spite of low vitality was that she was used to it. Three of the Mumford children had died in infancy.

A brilliant child, Catherine read the Bible through eight times before she was 12. She loved school and made high grades. But her school days were cut short by a severe spinal attack when she was only 14. This disease was so crippling she had to spend most of her time flat on her back.

Having to drop out of school was a keen disappointment, for she loved competition and wanted to lead the class.

However, since she couldn't go to school, she decided she would study theology—on her own. She poured over such volumes as Butler's *Analogy* and Finney's *Revival Lectures*. The Lord used these books to convict her of sin, and at 17 she openly received Christ as her Savior and Lord.

Her spinal condition had been improving, when a doctor examined her chest and discovered that she also had tuberculosis.

Soon she became so weak she couldn't leave the house. When plagued by a toothache, the dentist decided her pulse was too feeble to risk an extraction.

Faced with the possibility of never leaving her bed, Kate prayed that God would lead her into some useful occupation that would glorify Him. Soon she was convinced that the Lord was leading her to write letters—to win souls through correspondence. In the days that followed, letters filled with Gospel messages went to friends and relatives.

When she wasn't writing she was reading. In one 16-month period, while propped up in bed on a pillow, she read the Bible through twice in addition to the flood of letters she sent out.

Gradually her health improved enough so she could teach a Sunday school class. And so diligent was she with this undertaking that she spent two full days on each lesson. But her voice became so weak after each class, she frequently lost it completely for a day or two.

It was during this period that William Booth preached a trial sermon in their church and was accepted as pastor, the understanding being that Mr. Rabbitts would pay his salary.

Kate had hoped that marriage would end her illness. She engaged in Gospel work with utter abandon. Immediately following their marriage, the Booths went to Guernsey for special meetings. Huge throngs came. Hundreds were converted. But the excitement was too much—Kate was forced to return to her mother's home and go to bed.

This turn of events left her nearly crushed. Lying on her sickbed, her eyes filled; a feeling of complete frustration gripped her. It was then that her previous Bible reading came to her aid. Again and again she quoted Romans 8:28 to herself: "And we know that all things work together for good to them that love God, to them who are the called according to his purpose." The immediate problem, she decided, was to find God's will for her life—and to discover ways to make her illness an advantage rather than a handicap.

Soon the old pen was back in her hand and she was dashing off letters of encouragement to her husband and to others. And since she wrote from a sickbed rather than an ivory tower, her letters were received with unusual respect.

Throughout her life, her illnesses weren't always severe. There was never a time when she was completely well, yet there were times when she could get up and be about. During these periods she often engaged in house-to-house visitation campaigns, called on the sick, gathered clothes for the poor, urged people to take the temperance pledge, and did editorial work. And during those busy years she bore and raised eight children.

At a time of crisis, when evangelistic fields were being

closed to them by the conference under which they worked, Kate urged her husband to resign. This meant facing the world with no job, four children, and not a farthing to their names. But Kate declared she knew it was God's will and that He would see them through.

They moved to London without a call, and with no hint of an opening. Days went by and nothing turned up. There was no money, and their rent was due. Booth began to worry; but whenever he made a discouraging remark, Kate countered with a quotation from the Bible. Then there was a very small opportunity, and Kate declared it was a mandate from the Lord.

A campaign had been planned in Whitechapel—one of the poorest and vilest sections of London. A tent had been erected in an old Quaker burial ground. But illness had prevented the evangelist from coming. Since Booth was the only man the committee could think of, he was invited to do the preaching.

It would be better, they reasoned, to have him than no one!

The Booths accepted the challenge. Each evening as William preached, the crude benches were filled with drunkards, petty criminals, and paupers. There were conversions at almost every service; but it was useless to take up an offering, for these people had no money. The Booths, however, had to pay the bills and feed their children. What were they to do? Kate picked up her pen.

This time, instead of addressing individuals, she wrote newspaper articles about what her husband was doing. These colorful articles came to the attention of wealthy people, and before long the work that eventually became the Salvation Army was launched. Few decisions in regard to the Army were made without Kate's advice. Often this advice came from the sick room, as did dozens of articles for the "War Cry." Kate also designed the famous "Hallelujah bonnets" for the Army.

As the work grew, William Booth was often called away to conduct meetings. Kate never allowed her illnesses to interfere with these campaigns. The souls of others, as far as she was concerned, came before her rights as William's wife.

In Kate's 59th year, while Booth was at home, she returned from the doctor with shattering news. "He says that I have cancer and that I will only live for two years," she said, trying to sound cheerful.

Stunned, William Booth reached for a telegraph blank. "I'll cancel my meetings," he said.

"You will do no such thing!" she replied with the finality of a monarch. "There are people over there who are not ready to die; I am!"

On his return, William arranged for Kate to be taken to Clacton, where she could be by the sea she loved so much. People from all over the world came to the dying woman for counsel. She preached that a person could be down, but that he was never out. Her interest extended to all classes. She carried on a correspondence with Queen Victoria. But she also loved the convicts.

One day as she was nearing her death, she drew her daughter Evangeline to her side. She pleaded with her to remember the poor and needy and then added softly, "And, Eva, don't you forget that criminal you spoke to. Go to Lancaster jail and find him. Tell him your mother, when she was dying, prayed for him."

Her special concerns extended to all. She hoped the Army would continue to grow. Fearing some might be discouraged, she dictated a note for the "War Cry": "The waters are rising, but so am I. I am not going under, but over. Don't be concerned about your dying; only go on living well, and the dying will be all right."

The end came on October 4, 1890. She was 61. There had been a dreadful storm the night before. Flashes of jagged lightning had slashed through the air. But the morning was calm. The larks could be heard, and the beat of the waves on the shore was like the ceaseless pulsations of eternity.

As long as she could speak, she prayed and encouraged those at her bedside. Then, when she could no longer force words from her lips, she pointed to the motto on the wall. Those who followed her wasted finger read the words, "My grace is sufficient for thee."

14

"Let Us Go On"

David Livingstone leaned heavily against the goatskin nailed to the wall of his hut in Ujiji, and stared moodily across the busy market to the warm, distant hills. His shoulders were slumped, his eyes lackluster. The acute discouragement which he had fought against as he crisscrossed Africa now shared the mud bench with him, and was inching closer.

Rumors had come of a white man at Tabora, but Livingstone was too tired to be excited about them. It seemed that he had reached the end of his trail; that he would never discover the source of the Nile; that his last mission was a failure. His feet were ulcerated and refused to heal. His dysentery was getting worse. All but three of his porters had deserted. His last pair of shoes was in ribbons. His eyes were inflamed.

In addition to all of this, the bulk of his supplies had been stolen by a man he had trusted. There was not a yard of calico or a string of beads left. He had nothing to trade for food except his watch, his gun, and some extremely necessary instruments.

These troubles had reduced his usually hearty appetite. He had lost so much weight that he described himself in his journal as "being reduced to a skeleton."

Suddenly the sound of gunfire cut through the humid air. Livingstone shuddered. He hoped it was not another slaver killing and rounding up slaves for the Zanzibar market nearly a thousand miles away. But he had little time to think about it, for all at once his servant Susi came running up to him. "An Englishman!" he panted.

Livingstone smoothed his shabby gray trousers, and stepped into the open space in front of his hut to see what was going on. Soon a column of men approached. It was being led by a huge guide who carried a flag on the end of a spear. Right behind the burly African marched a strange white man wearing a new suit and freshly chalked helmet.

The population of Ujiji, attracted by something new, swarmed around the stranger and twisted curious eyes toward Livingstone.

Livingstone advanced to stand beneath the shade of a mango tree. The stranger's step now became more deliberate as he advanced between the two rows of wide-eyed, smiling Africans.

Removing his peaked helmet and bowing low, the stranger said, "Doctor Livingstone, I presume?"

"Yes," replied the doctor, returning the bow and lifting his consul's cap. This hat, with its faded gold band on a scarlet background, resembled a yacht cap, and was Livingstone's badge of authority as an English officer.

The two men shook hands, then the 58-year-old missionary suggested that they go to the wide veranda of his hut and escape the noon heat. Livingstone insisted that his visitor take his seat on the mud bench in front of the goatskin.

The new man introduced himself as Henry Morton Stanley. Livingstone, noticing his guest's porters nervously standing around with their loads, immediately suggested to Stanley that he should store his goods in his Ujiji home and move in with him. Stanley agreed to this.

Soon Stanley remembered that he had a bag of mail for Livingstone and sent a servant to fetch it. The doctor had not received any mail for two years and his hazel eyes gleamed when he saw the big stack. He glanced at a letter or two and then laid them down. He had gotten used to being without mail. The letters could wait for another hour or so.

While the sound of the surf from nearby Lake Tanganyika mingled with the gentle stir of the breeze in the palm trees, Stanley shared the latest news of the world. For the first time Livingstone learned that General Grant had been elected President of the United States; the Atlantic cable had been laid; his great friend, Lord Clarendon, had died; and that France had lost Alsace and Lorraine in her War of 1870 with Prussia.

As Livingstone listened to a voice that spoke clear English and that filled his blank years with news, he felt a new vigor coursing through his body. Time seemed to stand still as new hope gripped his spirit. Before he realized it, two of Stanley's servants were setting the table. They laid down a crimson cloth and set it with bright new silver, an excellent set of beautiful china, and a silver teapot brimming with the finest tea.

The servants began to come in with the food—a large kettle filled with porridge, stewed goat, curried chicken, meat cakes sent by the Arabs, yogurt, honey, fruit from Livingstone's kitchen, rice and dampers (small cakes of bread baked in hot ashes).

Livingstone faced this unexpected feast with an appetite and a joy he had not experienced in years. Bowing his head he prayed: "For what we are going to receive, make us, O Lord, sincerely thankful." He had barely finished the prayer when a well-filled fork was on its way to his mouth. He ate and ate in spite of the fact that most of his teeth were gone. Whenever Stanley paused with his steady flow of talk, Livingstone urged him to keep going, and between bites he would repeat over and over again, "You have brought me new life, you have brought me new life."

Livingstone's cook had become discouraged in trying to get him to eat. Now she slipped from the cookhouse and slyly watched as her master reached for more and more food. She was both astonished and delighted.

Finally, when it was quite late, Livingstone excused himself, saying that he wanted to read his mail. It was not until the next morning that he learned that Stanley had been sent out by James Gordon Bennett of the *New York Herald* to find him. Stanley did everything he could to help. He made great piles of all that he possessed—medicines, bales of calico, beads, and equipment—and divided it all between himself and Livingstone.

Doctor Livingstone had had no medicine of any kind for more than five years, and since his dysentery was becoming chronic, Stanley's gift of medicine was especially helpful. Stanley also set up a bath and spread out a Persian rug in order to make Livingstone comfortable. Livingstone was extremely grateful for all of this. Before Stanley came, he was picking at two meals a day. In explaining all of this to his daughter Agnes, he wrote: "The tears often come to my eyes on every fresh proof of kindness. My appetite returned . . ."

Soon Stanley began to urge Livingstone to go back to Scotland where his family and almost unlimited honor awaited him. While at home he could be fitted with artificial teeth, stir up lagging missionary interest—and rest. Stanley pleaded his cause well with all the youthful vigor of his thirty years, but Livingstone refused to even consider his proposals. Years before, he had written to his father-in-law, Robert Moffat: "I shall open up a path into the interior or perish. I have never had the shadow of a doubt as to the propriety of my course, and wish only that my exertions may be honored so far that the Gospel may be preached and believed in all this dark region."

One day, as Livingstone was sitting on his bench deep in thought, Stanley approached and said, "A penny for your thoughts, Doctor."

"They are not worth it, my young friend, and let me suggest that if I had any, possibly I would wish to keep them," replied Livingstone a little severely.

What were the thoughts which often caused David Livingstone to sit so quietly while he smiled, frowned, and moved his lips in silent conversation with himself? No one really knows. But there are many probabilities. Perhaps he was secretly considering Stanley's suggestion that he return to his home. As a doctor, he knew that he could not keep going without rest—that a year off might add several years to his life.

Doctor Livingstone's journeys had separated him from his children, and sometimes he was tempted to think that this separation was too high a price for what he was accomplishing. Frequently as he sat alone by a campfire after a long march, his mind went back to Shupanga, and he remembered his wife's last hours as she struggled with death on a crude bed made of boxes. The lines he wrote in his journal after her passing remained forever in his heart.

"It is the first heavy stroke I have suffered, and quite takes away my strength. I wept over her who well deserved my tears. I loved her when I married her, and the longer I lived with her I loved her the more. God pity the poor children . . . ."

Now, as he visited with Stanley, he wished that his Mary, the "Queen of the Wagons," could be with him. This was impossible, for her body was lying in its grave by the side of a huge baobab tree.

With the determination he had developed on a thousand marches, Livingstone pushed these things from his heart and joined in with Stanley's plans and laughter.

Since Livingstone had refused to return with him, Stanley decided to do the next best thing—the two of them would travel and explore together for awhile. They borrowed a large canoe from an Arab, placed the Stars and Stripes on the stern and the Union Jack on the bow, then started out with 16 men at the oars. Those were extremely happy days for Livingstone. He was even able to enjoy a good argument with Stanley over England's recent prime ministers; Stanley was for Disraeli, while Livingstone was for Gladstone!

Relaxing with his friend, who took care of the details, Livingstone talked about all sorts of things—especially the near future. Stanley especially remembered one of their conversations. "He told me that when he first obtains the privilege of sleeping in a four-poster bedstead, he cannot confine himself to one position in it but must try the luxury of rolling in it like a buffalo in his wallow, and then stretching himself diagonally, transversely, obliquely, and every other way, and sometimes with feet where head ought to be, or hanging over the sides."

Livingstone remembered the banquets he had had in England. Indeed, he often dreamed about them. To Stanley, he said, "You will think of me when you taste those marrow bones at the Geographical (Society) and the Devonshire cream." He was especially fond of marrow on toast.

Every earthly blessing, however, must have an end. After a long last conversation under the stars, Stanley and Livingstone went to bed, knowing that after breakfast in the morning they would have to part. Stanley wrote out in shorthand everything the doctor said.

At sunrise they faced each other over the breakfast table. On a different occasion they had had a great time at a similar meal, Livingstone drinking 13 cups of tea, while Stanley only managed 11. This time, however, their hearts were so full that neither one of them could manage a bite. Both men struggled with their tears. Livingstone knew his hour of decision had come. He could turn his back on Africa, be satisfied with his accomplishments, and return to England and honors with his friend.

But the lure of family, of health, or monetary rewards were not sufficient to divert him from the course he knew God had called him to follow. Many years before he had faced another crisis, and on that occasion he had gone through to victory. The story of that struggle was in his journals:

"14th January, 1856. Evening. Felt much turmoil of spirit in view of having all my plans for the welfare of this great region and teeming population knocked on the head by savages tomorrow. But I read that Jesus came and said, 'All authority in heaven and on earth has been given to me. Go therefore and make disciples of all nations . . . and lo I am with you always, to the close of the age.' It is the word of a gentleman of the most sacred and strictest honor, and there is an end to it. I will not cross furtively by night as I intended. It would appear as flight, and should such a man as I flee? Nay, verily, I shall take observations for latitude and longitude tonight, though they be my last. I feel quite calm now, thank God."

Finally, Stanley's men picked up their loads and began to sing. Livingstone walked by Stanley's side as the long caravan began its homeward journey. While climbing the low hills at the top of a valley, both men knew their days together were over. "Now, my doctor," said Stanley, his voice husky and at the breaking point, "you have come far enough and the sun is very hot. Let me beg of you to turn back."

Looking him full in the face, Livingstone replied, "I am grateful to you for what you have done for me. God guide you safely home, and bless you, my friend."

They shook hands, and the caravan continued on its journey. Doctor Livingstone watched until all but Stanley had disappeared over the hill. Then Stanley waved his handkerchief, and Livingstone responded by raising his hat. The day of parting was Thursday, March 14, 1872. No white man ever saw Livingstone again.

After thirty years of incredible hardship, Livingstone was on his last journey. But knowing that life was short, he shook off every hindrance and doggedly pressed on into the interior. He simply had to find and prove the source of the Nile! This discovery, he was certain, would open up Africa to the outside world and help put an end to slavery.

By the spring of 1873, the discoverer of Victoria Falls and a dozen other landmarks was nearing the end. This can be seen in his diary:

"April 15. Cross Lolotikila gain (where it is only fifty yards) by canoes . . . I, being very weak, had to be carried part of the way . . ."

"April 19. I am excessively weak, and but for the donkey, could not move a hundred yards. It is not all pleasure, this exploration . . ."

Livingstone's last surviving porter was Matthew Wellington, who lived in his little thatched hut just outside Mombasa. In a near-husky voice, he related, "Bwana Livingstone was always saying, 'Twende (Let us go on).'"

Wellington had special reasons for remembering and loving the doctor. As a boy he had been captured in what is now Tanzania and sold into slavery. While being shipped overseas for sale, the boat was captured by the British; he was rescued, and sent to India. After he had been enrolled in school at Nassick, he was chosen by Doctor Livingstone to return with him to Africa.

Upon his conversion in India, the boy had changed his name to Matthew; Livingstone had added the Wellington in honor of the victor of Waterloo.

After April 27, Livingstone was confined to his *kitanda* —the bed constructed by his porters. But riding on this crude bed made of poles and short sticks was not easy. Wellington remembered how Livingstone was constantly reminding him and others to be careful when they lifted him from the bed, for he could not stand any pressure on his back—especially in the lumbar region.

April 30 was damp and chilly, so a fire was built in front of Livingstone's hut, but Majwara was posted outside. He was instructed to call Susi or Chuma should Livingstone ask for something.

About 11 p.m. some villagers made a terrible racket as they drove a buffalo from their crops. "Is this the Luapula?" inquired Livingstone of Susi, after he had explained the noise.

"No, we are in Chitambo's village. . . ."

About an hour later, Livingstone summoned Susi and asked him to boil some water. Then he called for his medicine chest and selected a dose of calomel. Finally, he asked that a cup of water be placed by his bed and an empty cup next to it. This done, he murmured weakly, "All right, you can go now . . . ."

At about 4 a.m., Majwara summoned Susi. It seemed that Majwara had been overcome by drowsiness. But just before he had dozed off, he had noticed the Bwana kneeling by his bed. Majwara had no way of knowing how long he had slept. However, he was afraid that it was for a considerable time. When he opened his eyes, Livingstone was still on his knees. Susi summoned some others and they crept into the hut.

By the light of a small candle standing in its own wax on a crude chest, they could see their beloved leader. "He was bowed by the side of his bed, his body stretched forward, his head buried in his hands on the pillow," said Wellington.

One of the boys touched his cheek. It was cold.

In the morning, the porters had a solemn conference to discuss what they should do. None had any idea about how famous their friend was in the rest of the world. They just knew that he was a most unusual God-fearing man.

They decided that his body must be carried to the coast and put on a ship bound for England. They knew, of course, that the body would not keep that long. The problem was solved by Farijala. He had been a servant in a surgeon's house in Zanzibar and had seen many post-mortem examinations. With this knowledge, he removed Livingstone's internal organs and placed them in a tin box.

A hole was then dug for the tin box at the base of a smooth-barked myonga tree. Next, Jacob Wainwright read the burial service from the Anglican prayer book. Then the body was dried in the sun. While it was drying, Jacob Wainwright carved on the myonga tree: "Livingstone, May 4, 1873."

After the body had remained in the sun for two weeks, it was wrapped in calico and then fitted into a cylinder of bark that had been pried from a tree. The cylinder was then wrapped in an old sail and the bundle was attached to a long pole. Wellington and the others were afraid they might have difficulty with some of the tribes, for most of them were extremely superstitious about a dead body. Because of this, the men were very secretive about their burden. But they couldn't keep their secret forever.

Among the first to learn the truth was Chief Chitambo. He was most understanding and did not raise a complaint. Years later, he showed his respect by insisting that he be buried next to Livingstone's heart at the side of the myonga tree.

The porters knew that the task ahead of them was a hard one and a long one. But they did not shirk. After each camp, one of them would say, "Twende," and they would be on their way. They crossed rivers, climbed mountains, and made their way through fever-infested swamps, and scorching deserts. When trouble arose in Kasekera, they changed the shape of their bundle with mapira stalks, thus making it look like a bale of cotton. This reduced opposition to a mere grumble or two.

The entire journey to Zanzibar took nearly eleven months. There, the body was placed on the *H.M.S. Vulture* and shipped to England. On April 18th, Doctor Livingstone's body was buried in Westminster Abbey. It was a national day of mourning and the streets of London were black with those who had come to pay their respects.

Of the porters who had endured so much hardship, only one, Jacob Wainwright, was invited to accompany the body to England. Matthew Wellington was keenly disappointed, for he would have liked to have stood by the grave of his old friend. Nevertheless, he enjoyed a continuing honor denied the others. He lived to be a very old man, and as "Livingstone's Last Porter," he was enabled to inspire many a man with what he had seen with "his own eyes."

After Livingstone's death, historians discovered what is not an obvious fact. During all of those last incredible months David Livingstone was searching for the Nile in the wrong place! Chitambo's village was hundreds of miles too far to the south. In addition, the source of the Nile had already been discovered by John Hanning Speke in 1862 —over ten years before Livingstone's death.

Cynics might conclude that the Last Journey was a complete failure. But was it? On May 1—the day Susi and Chuma calculated Livingstone had died—a mighty blow was struck against slavery. On that memorable day, leaders of the Frere Mission were directed by the British Government to negotiate a treaty with the Sultan of Zanzibar—a treaty that would seal his ports to slavery. Also, on that day, the entire British naval patrol was ordered to stop all export of slaves from the entire coastal area. And on that same day the slave-market of Zanzibar was closed—forever!

But what was the force that caused the British Government to suddenly act like this? The answer is simple—public opinion. The story of a lonely missionary searching through Africa and refusing to return to honor and comfort with Stanley had gotten into the public conscience.

That God had something else in mind for Livingstone other than the discovery of the source of the Nile seems especially evident when we consider one absolutely incredible thing. Doctor Livingstone's journals—all of them—were preserved!

Today the source of the Nile means nothing; thousands see it every year. But those journals still breathe with the fervency of the Book of Acts. Indeed, those journals are worth the entire agony of Livingstone's most painful and discouraging hours. It would be almost impossible for a discouraged person to read those journals and remain discouraged.

No, they do not show the power of positive thinking. Instead, they show the power of God's thinking!

REACH OUT
with additional copies of this book...

Simply ask for them at your local bookstore—or order from the David C. Cook Publishing Co., Elgin, IL 60120 (in Canada: Weston, Ont. M9L 1T4).

---- **USE THIS COUPON** ----------------------

Name _____

Address _____

City _____ State _____ ZIP Code _____

TITLE	STOCK NO.	PRICE EA.	QTY.	SUB-TOTAL
Their Finest Hour	82917	$1.95		$

NOTE: On orders placed with David C. Cook Publishing Co., add handling charge of 25¢ for first dollar, plus 5¢ for each additional dollar.

Handling

TOTAL $ _____

DU

If you've just finished this book, we think you'll agree...

A COOK PAPERBACK IS

REWARDING READING

Try some more!

LOOK AT ME, PLEASE LOOK AT ME by Clark, Dahl and Gonzenbach. Accepting the retarded—with love—as told in the moving struggle of two women who learned how.
72595—$1.25

THE 13TH AMERICAN by Pastor Paul. Every 13th American is an alcoholic, and it could be anyone. A sensitive treatment of alcoholism by a minister who fought his way back.
72629—$1.50

THE EVIDENCE THAT CONVICTED AIDA SKRIPNIKOVA edited by Bourdeaux and Howard-Johnston. Religious persecution in Russia! The story of a young woman's courage.
72652—$1.25

LET'S SUCCEED WITH OUR TEENAGERS by Jay Kesler. Substitutes hope for parental despair—offers new understanding that exposes the roots of parent-child differences.
72660—$1.25

THE PROPHET OF WHEAT STREET by James English. Meet William Borders, a Southern Black educated at Northwestern University, who returned to lead the black church in Atlanta.
72678—$1.25

WHAT A WAY TO GO! by Bob Laurent. Your faith BEYOND church walls. Laurent says, "Christianity is not a religion, it's a relationship." Freedom, new life replace dull routine!
72728—$1.25

THE VIEW FROM A HEARSE (new enlarged edition) by Joseph Bayly. Examines suicide. Death can't be ignored— what is the Christian response? Hope as real as death.
73270—$1.25

WHAT'S SO GREAT ABOUT THE BIBLE (new enlarged edition) by James Hefley. Hefley presents the Bible as a literary miracle, an indestructible influence.
73288—$1.25

(Cont.)

MORE REWARDING READING

...from Cook

TELL ME AGAIN, LORD, I FORGET by Ruth Harms Calkin. Joyful poetry and sensitive drawings for sinkside musing, help on a drab winter day . . . with a way of turning gloom to gladness.
77263—$1.25

O CHRISTIAN! O JEW! by Paul Carlson. A Presbyterian pastor pens a book that is at once an odyssey for Christian readers—from Abraham to contemporary Israel—and a helpful guide to the ways, wit and wisdom of their Jewish friends. 272 pages.
75820—$1.95

BEYOND THE EXIT DOOR by Robert J. Vetter. Following his wife's untimely death, a family man draws on Divine strength for readjustment. Help for anyone facing the loss of a spouse.
77586—$1.25

LOVE MY CHILDREN by Dr. Rose B. Browne and James W. English. (Rev. ed.) A brilliant, highly educated black woman—dedicated to better teaching for the underprivileged—tells her story. 81828—$1.95

INVISIBLE HALOS by David C. Cook III. The president of a Sunday School publishing company introduces people who are for him unique, if unlikely, examples of Christianity in action.
77289—$1.50

Order books from your local bookstore . . . or David C. Cook Publishing Co., Elgin, IL 60120—in Canada: Weston, Ont. M9L 1T4. (On orders placed with David C. Cook Publishing Co., please add handling charge of 25¢ for the first dollar, plus 5¢ for each additional dollar.)

WHAT ABOUT HOROSCOPES? by Joseph Bayly. A topic on everyone's mind! As the author answers the question posed by the title, he also discusses witches, other occult subjects.
51490—95c

IS THERE HEALING POWER? by Karl Roebling. A keen interest in healing led the author to a quest of facts. A searching look at faith healers: Kathryn Kuhlman, Oral Roberts, others.
68460—95¢

SEX SENSE AND NONSENSE by James Hefley. Just what does the Bible say, and NOT say, about sex? A re-examination of common views—in the light of the Scriptures.
56135—95c

THE KENNEDY EXPLOSION by E. Russell Chandler. An exciting new method of lay evangelism boosts a tiny Florida church from 17 to 2,450 members. Over 50,000 copies sold.
63610—95¢

STRANGE THINGS ARE HAPPENING by Roger Ellwood. Takes you for a close look at what's happening in the world of Satanism and the occult today . . . and tells what it means.
68478—95c

You can order these books from your local bookstore, or from the David C. Cook Publishing Co., Elgin, IL 60120 (in Canada: Weston, Ont. M9L 1T4).

---------------**Use This Coupon**---------------

Name _____

Address _____

City _____ State _____ ZIP Code _____

TITLE	STOCK NO.	PRICE	QTY.	ITEM TOTAL
		$		$

	Sub-total $
NOTE: On orders placed with David C. Cook Publishing Co., add handling charge of 25¢ for first dollar, plus 5¢ for each additional dollar.	Handling _____
	TOTAL $ _____